Linux Networking Cookbook

Over 40 recipes to help you set up and configure
Linux networks

Gregory Boyce

PUBLISHING

BIRMINGHAM - MUMBAI

Linux Networking Cookbook

First published: June 2016

Production reference: 1220616

Published by Packt Publishing Ltd.
Livery Place
35 Livery Street
Birmingham B3 2PB, UK.

ISBN 978-1-78528-791-6

www.packtpub.com

Credits

Author
Gregory Boyce

Reviewer
Jean-Pol Landrain

Acquisition Editor
Sonali Vernekar

Content Development Editor
Onkar Wani

Technical Editor
Naveenkumar Jain

Copy Editor
Sneha Singh

Project Coordinator
Ulhas K

Proofreader
Safis Editing

Indexer
Hemangini Bari

Graphics
Kirk D'Penha

Production Coordinator
Shantanu N. Zagade

Cover Work
Shantanu N. Zagade

About the Author

Gregory Boyce is a technologist with nearly 20 years of experience in using and managing Linux systems. When he's not at work or spending time with his wife and two daughters, he is playing around with new technologies.

Gregory spent the last 15 years working at Akamai Technologies, where he has worked in roles ranging from Network Operations, Internal IT, Information Security, Software Testing, and Professional Services.

Currently, he heads up the Linux OS team that manages Akamai's custom Linux operating system, which runs on their massively distributed customer facing network.

I'd like to thank my wife, Vanessa, for all the support and Akamai for surrounding me with such a wonderful assortment of intelligent and interesting people.

About the Reviewer

Jean-Pol Landrain has a BSc degree in software engineering with a focus in network, real-time, and distributed computing. He gradually became a software architect with more than 18 years of experience in object-oriented programming, in particular with C++, Java/JEE, various application servers, and related technologies.

He works for Agile Partner, an IT consulting company based in Luxembourg. From early 2006 he became dedicated to the promotion, education, and application of agile development methodologies.

He has reviewed numerous books both for Manning and Packt Publishing about Docker, Git, Spring, and message-oriented middleware.

I would like to thank my fantastic wife, Marie, and my 9 year old daughter, Phoebe, for their daily patience regarding my passion for technology and the time I dedicate to it. I would also like to thank my friends and colleagues because a life dedicated to technology would be boring without the fun they bring to it.

www.PacktPub.com

eBooks, discount offers, and more

Did you know that Packt offers eBook versions of every book published, with PDF and ePub files available? You can upgrade to the eBook version at www.PacktPub.com and as a print book customer, you are entitled to a discount on the eBook copy. Get in touch with us at customercare@packtpub.com for more details.

At www.PacktPub.com, you can also read a collection of free technical articles, sign up for a range of free newsletters and receive exclusive discounts and offers on Packt books and eBooks.

https://www2.packtpub.com/books/subscription/packtlib

Do you need instant solutions to your IT questions? PacktLib is Packt's online digital book library. Here, you can search, access, and read Packt's entire library of books.

Why Subscribe?

- ▶ Fully searchable across every book published by Packt
- ▶ Copy and paste, print, and bookmark content
- ▶ On demand and accessible via a web browser

Table of Contents

Preface

Network administration is one of the main tasks of Linux system administration. By knowing how to configure system network interfaces in a reliable and optimal manner, Linux administrators can deploy and configure several network services including file, web, mail, and servers while working in large enterprise environments.

What this book covers

Chapter 1, Configuring a Router, starts by getting you to manually configure the IP address information on your system and then properly configure the system to bring up its interfaces automatically. From there, we'll move on to extending our system to act as a router for your own network, including DHCP for dynamically configuring client systems.

Chapter 2, Configuring DNS, will cover setting up your internal DNS server for both resolving external hostnames for you, as well as hosting DNS records for your own domain.

Chapter 3, Configuring IPv6, will provide a brief introduction of IPv6. We'll configure a tunnel to provide IPv6 connectivity, implement firewalling using iptables6, and provide IPv6 addresses to the rest of your network.

Chapter 4, Remote Access, will look at methods for remotely interacting with your new network using OpenSSH and OpenVPN.

Chapter 5, Web Servers, will set up web servers hosting PHP code, using both the Apache HTTPD server and NGINX.

Chapter 6, Directory Services, will tell us how to use Samba 4 to create an Active Directory-compatible directory service for your network.

Chapter 7, Setting up File Storage, will give us several options to explore for hosting your own file storage, including Samba, NFS, and WebDAV.

Chapter 8, Setting up E-mail, will tell us how to set up an e-mail server. We'll talk about how e-mail works as a service, set SMTP and IMAP mail services, and enable some spam filtering.

Chapter 9, Configuring XMPP, will tell us how to configure our own XMPP based IM service, configure it to communicate with other XMPP services, and configure Pidgin as a client to utilize the service.

Chapter 10, Monitoring Your Network, will tell us how to start monitoring services on our network using Nagios.

Chapter 11, Mapping Your Network, will cover mapping out the network in order to discover what is actually there.

Chapter 12, Watching Your Network, will cover watching over our network through centralized logging and managing an intrusion detection system using Snort.

What you need for this book

For this book you'll need a copy of Linux, preferably Ubuntu 14.04.

You'll also want access to three computers to install Linux on. One of the servers will need to have three network cards built into it.

For this purpose, I would strongly recommend using Virtual machines (VMs). Virtual Box will allow you to do this for free and is available on Windows, Linux, or OS X. You may find that the commercial offerings from VMWare, Parallels, or Microsoft may provide better performance, however.

Who this book is for

This book is targeted at Linux system administrators who have a good basic understanding and some prior experience of how a Linux machine operates, but want to better understand how various network services function, how to set them up, and how to secure them. You should be familiar with how to set up a Linux server and how to install additional software on them.

Conventions

In this book, you will find a number of text styles that distinguish between different kinds of information. Here are some examples of these styles and an explanation of their meaning.

Code words in text, database table names, folder names, filenames, file extensions, pathnames, dummy URLs, user input, and Twitter handles are shown as follows: "Modify `/etc/default/isc-dhcp-server` to add the interface which you should serve requests on."

A block of code is set as follows:

```
auto eth0
iface eth0 inet static
    address 10.0.0.1
    netmask 255.255.255.0
```

Any command-line input or output is written as follows:

```
# ip link set dev eth0 up
# ip link show eth0
```

New terms and **important words** are shown in bold. Words that you see on the screen, for example, in menus or dialog boxes, appear in the text like this: "Under **User Functions**, click **Create Regular Tunnel**. You may create up to 5 tunnels."

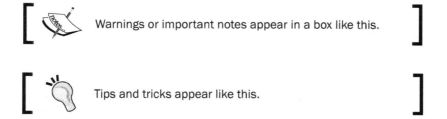

Warnings or important notes appear in a box like this.

Tips and tricks appear like this.

Reader feedback

Feedback from our readers is always welcome. Let us know what you think about this book—what you liked or disliked. Reader feedback is important for us as it helps us develop titles that you will really get the most out of.

To send us general feedback, simply e-mail `feedback@packtpub.com`, and mention the book's title in the subject of your message.

If there is a topic that you have expertise in and you are interested in either writing or contributing to a book, see our author guide at `www.packtpub.com/authors`.

Customer support

Now that you are the proud owner of a Packt book, we have a number of things to help you to get the most from your purchase.

Errata

Although we have taken every care to ensure the accuracy of our content, mistakes do happen. If you find a mistake in one of our books—maybe a mistake in the text or the code—we would be grateful if you could report this to us. By doing so, you can save other readers from frustration and help us improve subsequent versions of this book. If you find any errata, please report them by visiting http://www.packtpub.com/submit-errata, selecting your book, clicking on the **Errata Submission Form** link, and entering the details of your errata. Once your errata are verified, your submission will be accepted and the errata will be uploaded to our website or added to any list of existing errata under the Errata section of that title.

To view the previously submitted errata, go to https://www.packtpub.com/books/content/support and enter the name of the book in the search field. The required information will appear under the **Errata** section.

Piracy

Piracy of copyrighted material on the Internet is an ongoing problem across all media. At Packt, we take the protection of our copyright and licenses very seriously. If you come across any illegal copies of our works in any form on the Internet, please provide us with the location address or website name immediately so that we can pursue a remedy.

Please contact us at copyright@packtpub.com with a link to the suspected pirated material.

We appreciate your help in protecting our authors and our ability to bring you valuable content.

Questions

If you have a problem with any aspect of this book, you can contact us at questions@packtpub.com, and we will do our best to address the problem.

1
Configuring a Router

In this chapter, we will cover:

- ▸ Setting up the physical network
- ▸ Configuring IPv4
- ▸ Configuring IPv4 permanently
- ▸ Connecting two networks
- ▸ Enabling NAT to the outside
- ▸ Setting up DHCP
- ▸ Setting up a firewall with IPtables
- ▸ Setting up port forwarding
- ▸ Adding VLAN Tagging

Introduction

This chapter introduces some of the basic networking concepts and the methods to utilize them on Linux systems. It provides us with a good base to build upon. We're going to start with two computers connected with a single network cable and work our way from there to configure a router to connect your network to the Internet.

Routers are devices that are configured to span multiple networks and forward packets between them as needed. They also perform **Network Address Translation** (**NAT**) in order to allow your private network to share a single public IPv4 address.

Setting up the physical network

Before we start configuring the networking within Linux, we need to physically connect the systems. The simplest configuration involves connecting the two computers with a single cable, although connecting them to a switch may make more sense for additional expansion. Once physically connected, we need to confirm that they are working as expected.

How to do it...

On each Linux system, use the `ip` command to check for a network link as shown:

```
# ip link set dev eth0 up
# ip link show eth0
2: eth0: <BROADCAST,MULTICAST,UP,LOWER_UP> mtu 1500 qdisc pfifo_fast
state UP mode DEFAULT group default qlen 1000
    link/ether 00:0c:29:6e:8f:ab brd ff:ff:ff:ff:ff:ff
```

Some people may choose to use `ethtool`, `mii-tool`, or `mii-diag` to perform the same action.

Make sure to run the same command on both the systems, especially if you're connecting to a switch rather than directly connecting the two systems.

How it works...

The first command brings up the **network interface card** (**NIC**). This activates the interface and allows it to start the process to check for a network link or electrical connection between the two systems.

Next, the `show` command gives you a bunch of information about the link. You should see a *state* showing **UP**. If it shows **DOWN**, then you have a link issue of some sort. This could be a disconnected/bad cable, a bad switch, or you forgot to bring up the network interface.

Configuring IPv4

Now that we've established a link between the machines, let's put some IP addresses on the systems so that we can communicate between them. For now, let's look at manually configuring IP addresses rather than auto-configuring them via DHCP.

How to do it...

We need to manually configure the IP addresses using the `ip` command. Let's start with server 1:

```
# ip addr add dev eth0 10.0.0.1/24
# ip addr list eth0
2: eth0: <BROADCAST,MULTICAST,UP,LOWER_UP> mtu 1500 qdisc pfifo_fast
state UP group default qlen 1000
    link/ether 00:0c:29:6e:8f:ab brd ff:ff:ff:ff:ff:ff
    inet 10.0.0.1/24 brd 192.168.251.255 scope global eth0
       valid_lft forever preferred_lft forever
    inet6 fe80::20c:29ff:fe6e:8fab/64 scope link
       valid_lft forever preferred_lft forever
```

Now we need to perform the same action on server 2, but with 10.0.0.2/24 instead of 10.0.0.1/24.

How it works...

There are a few things in play here, so it probably makes sense to go through them one at a time.

First, let's start off by looking at the IP address that we're configuring. The 10.0.0.1 and 10.0.0.2 are a part of a series of netblocks set aside for private networks by RFC1918, IP Address Allocation for Private Internets. RFC1918 sets aside three large ranges, 10.0.0.0-10.255.255.255 (10.0.0.0/8), 172.16.0.0-172.31.255.255 (172.16.0.0/12), and 192.168.0.0-192.168.255.255 (192.168.0.0/16).

For our purpose, we're configuring 10.0.0.1/24, which is an IP range that includes 10.0.0.0-10.0.0.255. This includes 256 addresses, of which 254 are usable after setting aside 10.0.0.0 as the network address and 10.0.0.255 as the broadcast address. Both our systems get one IP in that range, which should allow them to communicate between them.

Next, we use the `ip` command to define an address on the `eth0` device using one of the IP addresses in that range. You need to make sure that each machine in that range has a different IP address in order to prevent IP address conflicts, which would make communication between the two systems impossible and communication with different systems difficult.

Some people may be accustomed to seeing the `ifconfig` command rather than the `ip` command used here. While it will certainly do the job in most cases, net-tool (and its `ifconfig` command) has been deprecated by most distributions since the turn of the century, in favor of `iproute2` and its `ip` command.

Once the commands have been run on both servers, you should be able to ping them from each other. Log in to 10.0.0.1 and run the following:

```
# ping -c 2 -n 10.0.0.2
```

If everything is configured properly, you will be able to see successful ping responses at this point.

Configuring IPv4 permanently

In the previous section we configured the network interface, but this configuration is only valid while the system is up and running. A reboot will clear this configuration, unless you take steps to make sure that it is configured on each boot. This configuration will be specific to the distribution that you are running, although most distributions fall under either the Debian or Red Hat methods.

How to do it...

Let' see how it works in Debian/Ubuntu:

1. Add eth0 configuration to `/etc/network/interfaces`:
   ```
   auto eth0
   iface eth0 inet static
       address 10.0.0.1
       netmask 255.255.255.0
   ```

2. Bring up the network interface:
   ```
   # ifup eth0
   ```

Let' see how it works in Red Hat/CentOS:

1. Add the eth0 configuration to `/etc/sysconfig/network-scripts/ifcfg-eth0`:
   ```
   DEVICE=eth0
   BOOTPROTO=none
   ONBOOT=yes
   NETWORK=10.0.0.0
   NETMASK=255.255.255.0
   IPADDR=10.0.0.1
   USERCTL=no
   ```

2. Bring up the network interface:

```
# ifup eth0
```

How it works...

Linux distributions are configured through `init` systems, such as Upstart, SystemD, or SysVInit. During the initialization process, the interfaces, or `ifcfg-eth0` files, are used as a configuration for the networking setup scripts. These scripts then use the same `ip` commands, or possibly `ifconfig` commands to set up and bring up the network interface.

Connecting two networks

For our next step, we're going to add a second interface to server 1. In addition to 10.0.0.1/24 being configured on `eth0`, we're going to configure 192.168.0.1/24 on `eth1`. The second interface could just as easily be 10.0.1.1/24, but let's make sure that the networks are obviously different.

The systems should be configured similar to Figure 1:

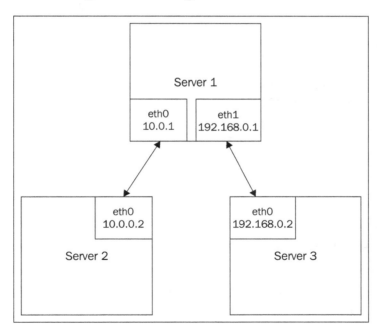

How to do it...

Let's connect two networks:

1. Configure the network interface on `eth1` on server 1:

   ```
   # ip link set dev eth1 up
   # ip addr add dev eth1 192.168.0.1/24
   # ip addr list eth1
   3: eth1: <BROADCAST,MULTICAST,UP,LOWER_UP> mtu 1500 qdisc pfifo_
   fast state UP group default qlen 1000
       link/ether 00:0c:29:99:ff:c1 brd ff:ff:ff:ff:ff:ff
       inet 192.168.0.1/24 scope global eth1
          valid_lft forever preferred_lft forever
       inet6 fe80::20c:29ff:fe99:ffc1/64 scope link
          valid_lft forever preferred_lft forever
   ```

2. Connect your third system to `eth1` on server 1.

3. Configure `eth0` on server 3 with an IP address of 192.168.0.2:

   ```
   # ip link set dev eth0 up
   # ip addr add dev eth0 192.168.0.2/24
   # ip addr list eth1
   3: eth0: <BROADCAST,MULTICAST,UP,LOWER_UP> mtu 1500 qdisc pfifo_
   fast state UP group default qlen 1000
       link/ether 00:0c:29:99:ff:c2 brd ff:ff:ff:ff:ff:ff
       inet 192.168.0.2/24 scope global eth1
          valid_lft forever preferred_lft forever
       inet6 fe80::20c:29ff:fe99:ffc1/64 scope link
          valid_lft forever preferred_lft forever
   ```

4. Add a default route on server 3:

   ```
   # ip route add default via 192.168.0.1
   ```

5. Enable routing on server 1:

   ```
   # echo net.ipv4.ip_forward=1 > /etc/sysctl.conf
   # sysctl -p /etc/sysctl.conf
   ```

6. Add a default route on server 2:

   ```
   # ip route add default via 10.0.0.1
   ```

How it works...

When you configure an IP address on a Linux system, you automatically have a route defined, which states that in order to access another IP address in the same subnet, you should use 0.0.0.0 as your gateway. This tells the IP stack that the system, if it exists, will be on the same layer as the two network segments, and that it should use ARP to determine the MAC address it should communicate with.

If you want to talk to a machine outside of that subnet, the system will need to know how to communicate with it. This is done by defining a route with a gateway IP address that you forward the packet to. You then depend on the gateway system to forward the packet to the correct destination.

Most commonly, you'll deal with a default route, which is the route that the system uses for any packet that is not deemed to be local. In our configuration, we tell the system that the default route is 192.168.0.1, which asks us to forward any non-local packets to an IP address configured on our server 1 box. This means that server 1 will act as our router.

You can also define more specific routes where you can explicitly define an IP address to forward packets to a specific IP address or subnet. This can be useful in a network where one router provides access to the Internet and a second router provides access to a second internal network.

At this point server 3, configured as 192.168.0.2, knows that IP addresses on 192.168.0.0/24 are local and any other packet should be sent to 192.168.0.1 in order to be forwarded. However, if you attempt to ping a system that is outside your local network (for example 10.0.0.2), it will not arrive. This is because routing on Linux systems is disabled by default and needs to be enabled on server 1 before it can forward packets. Enabling routing can be done by setting /proc/sys/net/ipv4/ip_forward to 1, or via sysctl, which is the manner in which we've chosen to set it.

Once routing is enabled, packets addressed from server 3 will be received by your router and forwarded to 10.0.0.2 (server 2) via eth0 on the router. 10.0.0.2 will receive the packet from your router and promptly attempt to respond. This response will fail, as server 2 does not have a defined route for accessing the 192.168.0.1/24 network. This is fixed by adding a default route on server 2 as well, but sending to the router's interface on the 10.0.0.0/24 network.

Now server 3 knows how to address server 2, server 2 knows how to address server 3, and server 1 routes packets between the two as needed. Congratulations, you have connected two networks.

Enabling NAT to the outside

Connecting two local networks is useful, but these days it's more common to want to connect a local network to the Internet. The basic concept works the same, but with the necessary addition of NAT. NAT rewrites your packet headers in order to make them appear as if they come from your router, thus effectively hiding your system's address from the destination.

How to do it...

Create a third NIC (`eth2`) on server 1 and connect it to your cable modem or ISP's router.

1. Configure `eth2` to receive an IP address via DHCP:

   ```
   auto eth2
   iface eth2 inet dhcp
   ```

2. Use `iptables` to enable NAT on packets heading out through `eth2`:

   ```
   # /sbin/iptables -t nat -A POSTROUTING -o eth2 \
     -j MASQUERADE
   # /sbin/iptables -A FORWARD -i eth2 -o eth0 -m \
     state --state RELATED,ESTABLISHED -j ACCEPT
   # /sbin/iptables -A FORWARD -i eth0 -o eth2 -j ACCE PT
   ```

How it works...

In the last section, we discussed how in order for two systems on different networks to be able to talk to each other, they need to have routes defined which will forward packets to a router that can deliver the packet to the appropriate destination. The same is true on the Internet.

If server 2 attempts to contact an IP address on the Internet, for example Google's nameserver at 8.8.8.8, your router will pass them onto the destination. Let's give that a try:

```
# ping -c 2 8.8.8.8
PING 8.8.8.9 (8.8.8.8) 56(84) bytes of data.
--- 8.8.8.8 ping statistics ---
2 packets transmitted, 0 received, 100% packet loss, time 999ms
```

No responses were received. So what went wrong here?

You'll recall that I said the IP addresses that we were using were defined by RFC1918 as internal IP address space. Due to this, these IP addresses are not directly usable as Internet hosts. In our example, one of the two following things will happen:

- Our router will send packets out of the Internet-facing interface, where it will travel across the Internet to our destination, which will respond to the packet. The response will not be able to find its way back to our system due to the un-routed nature of the destination.

- Our router will send the packets out of its Internet-facing interface, where the next hop will drop the packets due to implementing egress filtering of traffic with invalid source addresses.

Iptables is a command-line tool in Linux for interfacing with the Linux kernel firewall, which is implemented as a part of the netfilter subsystem.

Let's break down the first command line:

- The -t option specifies the packet matching table to use. In this case, we're going to use the nat table.

- f-A indicates that the specified rule should be appended to the selected chain, which in this case is POSTROUTING. The POSTROUTING chain is processed after the kernel handles packet routing.

- -o specifies the output interface. In our example, the eth0 interface contains the internal IP systems and eth2 leads to the Internet.

- -j specifies what to do if the packet matches the rule. In this case, we're going to masquerade the packet (modify the IP).

Put them together and we have matching packets heading out on eth2; rewrite the source IP address and track it in the NAT table.

The second command is added in the -m command, which matches a packet property, in this case state. For the packets that came in on eth1 (from the Internet), and destined to eth0 (lan), check to see if they are related to or are a part of an established connection. If so, accept the packet and assign it to the FORWARD chain. The FORWARD chain handles any packet that is being passed through your router rather than the packets originating from the system (OUTPUT chain) or packets destined to your system (INPUT chain).

Finally, any packets that come in on eth0 (lan) and are heading out on eth2 (Internet) are just automatically accepted.

Setting up DHCP

You now have a router that provides Internet access to all systems behind it, but the systems behind it need to be manually configured with IP addresses while avoiding conflicts. You also need to configure them with DNS servers for resolving host information. To solve this, we're going to configure a DHCP server on your router to be responsible for handing out addresses.

Dynamic Host Configuration Protocol (**DHCP**) allows you to centralize your IP address management. Machines which are added to a network will issue a DHCP request asking any available DHCP server to provide it with configuration information including IP address, subnet mask, gateway, DNS server, and so on.

How to do it...

Let's set up DHCP in Debian/Ubuntu:

1. Install a DHCP server:

   ```
   # sudo apt-get install isc-dhcp-server
   ```

2. Modify /etc/default/isc-dhcp-server to add the interface which you should serve requests on:

   ```
   # sudo sed -i "s/^INTERFACES.*/INTERFACES="eth0"\
     /etc/default/isc-dhcp-server
   ```

3. Modify /etc/dhcp3/dhcpd.conf to configure the network information you want to serve:

   ```
   ddns-update-style none;
   option domain-name "example.org";
   option domain-name-servers 8.8.8.8, 8.8.4.4;
   default-lease-time 600;
   max-lease-time 7200;
   authoritative;

   subnet 10.0.0.0 netmask 255.255.255.0 {
     range 10.0.0.10 10.0.0.100;
     option routers 10.0.0.1;
   }
   ```

Let's set up DHCP in Red Hat/CentOS

1. Install a DHCP server:

   ```
   # sudo yum install dhcp
   ```

2. Modify /etc/dhcp/dhcpd.conf to configure the network information you want to serve:

   ```
   ddns-update-style none;
   option domain-name "example.org";
   option domain-name-servers 8.8.8.8, 8.8.4.4;
   default-lease-time 600;
   max-lease-time 7200;
   authoritative;

   subnet 10.0.0.0 netmask 255.255.255.0 {
     range 10.0.0.10 10.0.0.100;
     option routers 10.0.0.1;
   }
   ```

How it works...

The first thing you might notice about the difference between Debian-and Red Hat-based systems is that in Debian-based systems, you need to explicitly define the interfaces to listen on, while this is not needed on Red Hat systems. This is because Red Hat has chosen to trust ISC DHCP's built-in restriction to only listen on interfaces that have an IP address in the same subnet as DHCP leases were set up for.

Let's look at the configuration for the DHCP server itself.

The first section defines the global configuration parameters:

- ▶ ddns-update-style: This defines optional functionality to update a DNS server with hostnames for the machines in your network. We'll look at this option in detail later in the book.

- ▶ option domain-name: This defines the domain name for your network. On Linux DHCP clients, this populates the **search** field that specifies the domain to search in for non-fully qualified domain names.

- ▶ option domain-name-servers: This specifies the default DNS servers, which your clients should use for domain resolution. In this example, we've used Google's public nameserver, but you may instead want to use your ISP's nameservers or a different public service.

- ▶ `Max-lease-time` and `default-lease-time`: This defines how many seconds the IP address can dedicate to the requesting machine. Clients can also request for a specific lease length. Max-lease-time puts a cap on how long they can request it for, while default-lease-time comes into play if they don't request a specific lease length. Longer leases cut down on the number of IP address changes you may experience, while shorter leases make sure that you don't run out of IP addresses if you have a lot of short-term users on the network.

- ▶ `authoritative directive`: This tells the DHCP server that it is the authority for this particular network. Sometimes, clients that have recently had a lease on another network may attempt to re-request the same IP address. An authoritative server may send them a DHCPNAK (negative acknowledgement) to tell them that they must request a new IP address. If your DHCP server is not the only one on the network, you may set it as not authoritative in order to avoid this behavior.

The second section is the subnet declaration. Your DHCP server must know about all the subnets configured on the interface that it has been told to serve DHCP addresses on. For the subnets on which it should serve addresses, you should define the range of IPs to hand out and you most likely want to define your network gateway as well. If your machine has multiple IP addresses on the interface and you only want to serve IPs to one of them, you should still define the subnet, but leave out the range and gateway information from within the brackets. For example:

```
subnet 10.0.0.0 netmask 255.255.255.0 {
}
```

Now that your DHCP server is configured, it will automatically hand out the IP addresses to all machines that connect to the network which are configured to request addresses via the DHCP protocol, which is often the default. It will keep track of these leases in a human-readable format in `/var/lib/dhcpd/dhcpd.leases`, in order to avoid having multiple machines receive the same address.

Setting up a firewall with IPtables

We touched upon `iptables` a little while discussing NAT, but now we're going to go a bit deeper into configuring a secure firewall for your network.

How to do it...

A properly configured firewall should be configured in a default deny configuration with specific allows (Whitelist) for what you want to accept:

```
# iptables -A INPUT -i lo -j ACCEPT
# iptables -A INPUT -m state --state ESTABLISHED,RELATED -j ACCEPT
# iptables -A INPUT -p tcp --dport 22 -j ACCEPT
```

```
# iptables -P INPUT DROP
# iptables -P FORWARD DROP
# iptables -P OUTPUT ACCEPT
# iptables -A FORWARD -i eth0 -j ACCEPT
# iptables -t nat -A POSTROUTING -o eth2 \
-j MASQUERADE
# iptables -A FORWARD -i eth2 -o eth0 -m \
state --state RELATED,ESTABLISHED -j ACCEPT
# iptables -A FORWARD -i eth0 -j ACCEPT
```

How it works...

We start off by setting an **ACCEPT** policy on traffic destined to the local system on the localhost adapter (`-i lo`). A lot of software expects to be able to communicate over the localhost adapter, so we want to make sure we don't inadvertently filter it.

Next, we set an **ACCEPT** policy for any packet that matches a state (`-m` state) of ESTABLISHED, RELATED. This command accepts packets which are a part of, or related to, an established connection. ESTABLISHED should be pretty straightforward. RELATED packets are special cases that the connection tracking module needs to have a prior knowledge of. An example of this is the FTP protocol operating in active mode. The FTP client in active mode connects to the server on port 21. Data transfers however, operate on a second connection originating from the ftp server from port 20. During the operation of the connection, the port 21 packets are ESTABLISHED, while the port 20 packets are RELATED.

The third command accepts any TCP connection (`-p tcp`) destined for port 22 (`--dport 22`) that is destined for your system. This rule allows you to SSH into the machine.

Next, we will define the default policies. By default, we drop packets on the INPUT and FORWARD chains and accept packets on the OUTPUT chain.

The last three lines you'll recognize from the NAT section, which tells the firewall to allow any packets starting on the internal network and heading out to the Internet.

Additional **ACCEPT** rules based upon destination ports can be opened as needed as INPUT lines, like the port 22 one.

Setting up port forwarding

In the previous section, we configured `iptables` to accept connections to port 22 in order to allow people to SSH into the host. Sometimes, you want to forward a port to a system behind the firewall instead of having the service run on the firewall itself. For example, you may have a web server running on port 8080 on an internal box that you want to expose to the Internet via port 80 on the firewall.

How to do it...

1. Rewrite packets addressed to port 80 to instead go to port 8080:

   ```
   # iptables -t nat -A PREROUTING -p tcp -i eth2 --dport 80 \
   -j DNAT --to-destination 192.168.0.200:8080
   ```

2. Accept any packets addressed to 192.168.0.200 port 8080:

   ```
   # iptables -A FORWARD -p tcp -d 192.168.0.200 \
   --dport 8080 -m state --state NEW,ESTABLISHED,RELATED \
   -j ACCEPT
   ```

How it works...

This example is a lot simpler since it builds upon concepts we've already learned. We just have two simple commands:

▶ First we set up a PREROUTING rule which will be processed once the packet is received, prior to any routing rules being applied. If the packet is TCP and came in on the Internet interface (eth2) with a destination port, then the packet is added to the destination NAT (DNAT) chain with a final destination of 192.168.0.200 port 8080.

▶ Next, any packet destined for 192.168.0.200 port 8080 is either a new connection or an established connection; the packet is then accepted for forwarding to the destination.

Adding VLAN Tagging

Right now we have a rather simple network configuration. We have a single router with a public-facing IP address on one interface and a private IP address on the second interface. But what if we want to have multiple private networks behind the route?

Our first option in this scenario would be to add additional IP addresses to the internal interface. The ip command allows you to assign multiple IPs to a single interface, with optional interface aliases like eth0:0. This will allow you to assign IP addresses to systems behind the firewall within one of the few ranges and have them all route appropriately.

The downside of this approach is that all the internal IPs exist within the same collision domain of the network. This has a few implications, including the ability to move systems between those IP ranges and potentially bypassing access control rules, as well as problems assigning addresses via DHCP due to confusion about what address range to hand out.

The second option would be to put a third network card in the router and then either plug the additional card into a dedicated switch or separate out the existing switch into multiple VLANs and plugging the new network card into a port on a dedicated VLAN for that network. The downside here is the additional cost of the NIC (assuming you have space to add it) and then either the usage of an extra switch port or an extra switch.

The third option is to configure the switch into dedicated VLANs and plug the LAN side of your router into a port configured as a trunk. From there, Linux can be configured to use VLAN tagging to split your single physical interface into a pair of virtual interfaces and tag packets, as appropriate, so that the switch automatically adds them to the appropriate VLAN.

How to do it...

There are two steps required in order to use VLAN tagging on your Linux server:

1. The first is to hook it up to a switch that has VLAN enabled, connected to a port which is allowed to act as a trunk. The specifics around how to configure a switch in this mode are outside of the scope of this book, since they are specific to the switch itself. You'll want to find a managed switch which supports the 802.1Q standard and consult its documentation for configuration.

2. The second thing you'll need is to create virtual interfaces assigned to the desired `VLAN`. In our case, we're going to create two virtual interfaces, which are assigned to `vlans` 1 and 2.

```
# ip link add link eth0 name eth0.1 type vlan id 1
# ip link add link eth0 name eth0.2 type vlan id 2
```

Now that they exist, you can treat them like normal network interfaces and configure them as we did in the section on adding a second network.

> Note that `eth0.1` is a naming convention, not a requirement at this point. You could instead choose to name the interfaces names *wireless* and *wired* if you wanted to.

Making this change permanent can be rather distribution specific and may depend on the use of the `vconfig` command, which is distributed through the VLAN package on Debian/ Ubuntu. Debian-based distributions will automatically create VLAN interfaces if you specify an interface in `/etc/network/interfaces` which is named as a physical interface, followed by a period, and then a VLAN ID, as `eth0.1` is our example.

How it works...

VLAN tagging, as defined by the 802.1Q standard, functions at the Ethernet layer level. A standard Ethernet frame contains 4 fields, the destination MAC address, the source MAC address, the EtherType or length field (depending on the type of frame), the data (the IP packet), and a frame check sequence (FCS). 802.1Q works by adding a VLAN tag between the source MAC address and then the EtherType/length field.

A switch that supports 802.1Q may have one or more network ports that are configured to act as a **Trunk**. Trunk ports will accept VLAN tagged packets and will pass them along as appropriate. They will detect the specified VLAN tag, determine the appropriate VLAN the packet is destined to, and will deliver the packet to any switch ports that are on that VLAN. Tagged packets can even pass between multiple switches as long as they are properly configured. If a packet is received without a tag on it, it will have a tag added automatically, based upon the VLAN associated with the switch port it was received on.

2
Configuring DNS

In this chapter, we will cover:

- ▸ Setting up your system to talk to a nameserver
- ▸ Setting up a local recursive resolver
- ▸ Configuring dynamic DNS on your local network
- ▸ Setting up a nameserver for your public domain
- ▸ Setting up a slave nameservers

Introduction

This chapter introduces the **Domain Name System** (**DNS**). You'll learn what DNS is, how it works, and how to configure it to work according to your requirements. We'll start by configuring your machines to be able to resolve hostnames, such as `www.google.com` and we'll work toward learning to configure your own domain.

Setting up your system to talk to a nameserver

In the previous chapter, we did some basic testing of your network connection by pinging other hosts by IP address directly. However, I'm sure you'd rather not visit web pages by requesting them by IP address, rather than by the domain name. This problem is solved using a recursive DNS server to resolve the hostnames into IP addresses, which your computer can then connect to.

How to do it...

Let's set up a DNS server to resolve the hostnames into IP addresses:

1. Configuring Linux to use a DNS server is very easy. Just add a single line to `/etc/resolv.conf`:

   `nameserver 8.8.8.8`

2. You may also want to add a *domain* line, which will allow you to access things by their hostname rather than by their **fully qualified domain name** (**FQDN**). For example, domain `example.org` in `resolv.conf` will allow you to ping `mail.example.org` as just *mail*.

If your system uses DHCP for receiving its IP address, then the content of this file can be managed through the configuration of the DHCP server. This makes easier management of nameserver IPs and domains on your network possible.

How it works...

The nameserver line in `/etc/resolv.conf` provides the IP address of a nameserver that your system is allowed to query against. In this particular example, we're using 8.8.8.8, which is a publicly available recursive DNS server owned and operated by Google. You may also want to consider using a nameserver provided by OpenDNS or one provided by your ISP. A properly configured recursive nameserver is restricted to only allow queries from the intended users, so you'll want to make sure that you're either using one intended for the general public or one intended specifically for you.

When your system attempts to contact a site, such as `www.example.org`, the browser will attempt to see if the matching IP address already exists in the browser's hostname cache.

If it does not, it issues a `gethostbyname` request to the local C library, which then checks its local configuration in `/etc/nsswitch.conf` to determine how lookups should be performed. You may find something similar to `hosts: files dns` in that file, which indicates that for finding host information, you should first look at local files, such as `/etc/hosts`, and you should check DNS if that fails.

Assuming that you didn't have a matching entry in `/etc/hosts`, your C library's stub DNS resolver will look in `/etc/resolv.conf` for the IP address of your DNS server and will then send a DNS query with recursion enabled over UDP port 53 to the listed DNS server. The server will check its local cache for an answer and will issue queries to the various authoritative nameservers, starting with the nameservers of the DNS root (`.`), followed by org, and then finally, example. The nameservers, for example, will pass back the IP address associated with `www.example.org` to your recursive nameserver, which will then pass it back to you.

Setting up a local recursive resolver

Since all attempts to access a website require that you look up the hostname, the responsiveness of your nameserver can have a large impact on the loading of a webpage. A slow nameserver can delay the initial loading of the webpage as well as the loading of the various embedded images, video, and JavaScript, which might have been pulled third-party sites.

In this section, we'll be looking at setting up our own recursive nameserver, which will help cut down on the round trips between you and your resolver. We will additionally configure it to forward uncached queries to a public recursive nameserver in order to take advantage of their caching.

How to do it...

Let's set up the local recursive resolver:

1. Install `bind9` on Ubuntu; this can be done with `sudo apt-get install bind9`. On Red Hat and CentOS, it can be done with `yum install bind` instead. For other distributions, consult the relevant documentation.

2. Add an `allow-recursion` entry in the options section of the `bind9` configuration in order to prevent it from being used for denial of service attacks:

```
allow-recursion {
192.168.1.0/24;
"localhost;"
};
```

3. Consider listening to only your internal IP address with the following option:

```
listen-on {
   192.168.1.1;
};
```

4. If you want to use a `forwarders`, add the following to your options section:

```
forwarders {
8.8.8.8;
8.8.4.4;
};
```

How it works...

While your mileage may vary from distribution to distribution, `bind9` is often distributed with a default configuration that acts as a recursive nameserver with no restrictions on who can issue queries against it. This sort of configuration can be abused by people looking to perform a DNS-based amplified denial of service attack by sending you a spoofed UDP packet containing a request, which results in a large response. This causes you and a large number of other servers to send the large responses to the DoS target.

The `allow-recursion` setting that we've provided tells `bind9` to only answer to recursive queries from your local network and the special *localhost* variable that includes all IP addresses configured on the server itself. Once this setting is in place, the server will respond to these queries with a short *refused* response rather than a potentially large data response.

`listen-on` takes restrictions one step further by allowing you to tell the server to not bind to particular network interfaces at all. If you're running on a router with multiple interfaces, you can choose to have `bind9` to only listen on the internal interface. Depending on your firewall configuration, this means that someone sending a request on an external interface will either get an ICMP destination port unreachable message or no response at all.

Finally, the forwarders' setting configures a list of DNS servers that you can go to in the event that it does not already have an entry cached. In this case, we're using the two public Google servers again, but you can choose to use your ISP's nameservers instead.

There's more...

There's one additional piece of information that is very useful to know if you are planning on running your own DNS server. As previously noted, the DNS protocol typically operates over UDP port 53. This is due to the low overhead nature of the UDP protocol, which does not require any sort of handshake to create and then tear down the connections. Over UDP, DNS is able to issue a single packet for a request and mostly receive a single packet as a response.

You may note that I said typically. Due to a limit on the maximum size of a UDP DNS request or response packet, the protocol can switch to TCP instead. The maximum size of a DNS request/response is 512 bytes unless EDNS0 is being used to increase the size to 4096 bytes. Any packet larger than those sizes will trigger a switch from UDP to TCP by the server sending a partial packet with the truncated bit set.

While a majority of DNS traffic that you'll see will be UDP, keep in mind that during troubleshooting and firewall rule writing, you may see TCP as well.

Configuring dynamic DNS on your local network

Right now you get your IP address configured automatically via DHCP and you're able to resolve DNS records from the internet via your DNS server. With the use of Dynamic DNS, you can also leverage your DNS server to address your local systems by name as well.

How to do it...

Let's configure dynamic DNS on your local network:

1. First, we need to configure your bind instance to host DNS for your internal domain, as well as reverse DNS for your IP range. For our example, we'll use a domain of `example.org`:

```
zone "example.org" {
  type master;
  notify no;
  file "/var/lib/bind/example.org.db";
}
zone "0.168.192.in-addr.arpa" {
  type master;
  notify no;
  file "/var/lib/bind/rev.1.168.192.in-addr.arpa";
};
```

2. Next we populate the zone in `example.org.db`:

```
example.org.  IN  SOA  router.example.org. admin.example.org. (
  2015081401
  28800
  3600
  604800
  38400
)
example.org.    IN    NS    ns1.example.org.
router    IN    A    192.168.1.1
```

3. Then we populate the reverse zone in `rev.1.168.192.in-addr.arpa`:

```
@ IN SOA ns1.example.org. admin.example.org. (
   2006081401
   28800
   604800
   604800
   86400
)
IN    NS     ns1.example.org.
1                     IN    PTR    router.example.org.
```

4. In order to connect the DHCP and DNS services, we need to generate a HMAC key for securing the communication. This can be completed by executing `dnssec-keygen -a HMAC-SHA512 -b 512 -r /dev/urandom -n USER DDNS`. This command will generate a pair of files named `Kddns_update.+NNN+NNNNN.private` and `Kddns_update.+NNN+NNNNN.key`.

5. Create a file called `ddns.key` and insert the following content with `<key>` replaced by the string marked `Key:` in the `.private` file:

```
key DDNS {
   algorithm HMAC-SHA512;
   secret "<key>";
};
```

6. Copy `ddns.key` to both `/etc/dhcp` and `/etc/bind` with the proper permissions using the following:

```
# install -o root -g bind -m 0640 ddns.key \
/etc/bind/ddns.key
# install -o root -g root -m 0640 ddns.key \
/etc/dhcp/ddns.key
```

7. Tell bind about the DDNS updating key by adding it to `/etc/bind/named.conf.local`:

```
include "/etc/bind/ddns.key";
```

8. Then tell bind to allow updating of the zones you previously created by adding an allow-update entry to your zones so that they look similar to the following:

```
zone "example.org" {
   type master;
   notify no;
   file "/var/lib/bind/example.org.db";
   allow-update { key DDNS; };
}
```

9. Now we need to update the DHCP server to have it hand out your nameserver instead of Google's and send hostname updates to your DNS server using the correct key:

```
option domain-name "example.org";
option domain-name-servers 192.168.1.1;
default-lease-time 600;
max-lease-time 7200;
authoritative;
ddns-updates          on;
ddns-update-style     interim;
ignore                client-updates;
update-static-leases  on;
include "/etc/dhcp/ddns.key";

subnet 10.0.0.0 netmask 255.255.255.0 {
  range 10.0.0.10 10.0.0.100;
  option routers 10.0.0.1;
}
zone EXAMPLE.ORG. {
  primary 127.0.0.1;
  key DDNS;
}

zone 2.168.192.in-addr.arpa. {
  primary 127.0.0.1;
  key DDNS;
}
```

How it works...

Bind/named supports the ability to dynamically update DNS records through the use of clients, which are configured to sign the update messages using HMAC. The server is able to validate the authenticity of the messages by performing the same hashing operation that the client had performed with the same shared key. If the hash value sent by the client with the message matches the hash value calculated locally by the server, then we know that the client and server both have the same shared key.

This dynamic update feature can be leveraged to create/modify DNS records on the fly using the nsupdate command. In our case, we're going to have ISC DHCPD send the update commands directly, as new hosts are found.

As a system requests an IP address through the DHCP protocol, the client includes its hostname as a part of the initial discovery request. This hostname is recorded as a part of the lease. When ISC DHCP is set up for DDNS, it issues a DNS update request to the configured DNS server. Now your system is resolvable by other clients, at least until its lease expires.

Setting up a nameserver for your public domain

Setting up a nameserver for a public domain works the same way as setting up a DNS server for an internal hostname, just with a few additional parts that we'll want to make sure are in a good state.

How to do it...

Let's set up a nameserver for a public domain:

1. Set up a properly configured SOA record:

```
example.org.  IN  SOA  ns1.example.org. admin.example.org. (
  2015081401
  28800
  3600
  604800
  38400
  )
```

2. Set up a record for NS hosts:

```
Ns1     IN      A       192.168.1.1
```

3. Set up glue records:

```
$ORIGIN example.org
        IN      NS      ns1.example.org.
Ns1     IN      A       192.168.1.1
```

How it works...

The first step is to configure the **start of authority (SOA)** for your domain. The SOA provides basic information about the zone itself. It contains a number of fields, including:

▶   Example.org: The zone.

▶   IN: Class of the record. IN is Internet, which you'll see for the majority of DNS records that you see.

- ► SOA: Start of authority.

- ► `ns1.example.org`: This is the primary/master DNS server for the zone.

- ► `admin.example.org`: This is the responsible party for the domain. This should be an e-mail address with the `@` character changed to a (`.`). So in this example, `admin@example.org` should be contactable.

- ► `2015081401`: This is the serial number of the zone. This is a 32-bit integer, which should increment when the zone changes. If the primary DNS server is not configured to notify slaves of changes, the slaves will automatically perform a zone transfer when this value increases. Using a numeric date for the serial is a common practice.

- ► `28800`: This is the refresh period. It defines how often a slave should contact the master in order to check for updates of the serial number. You might see warnings if this value is less than 20 minutes or greater than 12 hours.

- ► `3600`: Retry period. If a slave server cannot contact its master, how often should it retry?

- ► `604800`: Expire period. If retries have failed beyond this period of time, the slave server will stop acting as an authority for the domain.

- ► `38400`: This is the minimum/default TTL value. According to the RFC, this defines the lowest possible TTL value for a record in the zone. In practice, most DNS server implementations treat this as the default TTL value for records which do not set it explicitly.

The next two items define the same information in two separate places. NS records point to the *A* record for the DNS server, which is authoritative for the zone. For example, ns1.example.org is authoritative for the example.org zone. That, however, leaves a bootstrapping problem in which the A record for `ns1.example.org` is defined within the `example.org` zone file.

The solution for this bootstrapping issue is to use glue records. Glue records are stub records that exist at the point of delegation and define NS records for a zone as well as their matching A records. These values will be overridden by the records provided by the zone itself.

A good example of glue records comes when you register a domain. In our example domain, example.org is delegated by the `.org` DNS infrastructure. Your domain registrar should provide you with a mechanism to add NS records and their matching A records on the `.org` servers.

Since the glue records are managed outside of your zone, they're very easy to neglect when updating your DNS infrastructure. If your name servers are changing, you'll want to change them in the zone as well as in the glue records.

Setting up a slave nameserver

The nameserver infrastructure that we've configured so far is sufficient to get the domain to function, but it is currently a single point of failure. In order to deal with your existing nameserver being unreachable for some reason, we're going to want to add at least one additional nameserver for your network.

Now, maybe your initial thought would be to configure the nameservers identically and create some method to synchronize the zone files across the systems. Luckily, this isn't needed. Rather, bind/named can handle the synchronization internally, through the use of zone transfer (AXFR) requests or incremental zone transfer (IXFR) requests secured with the same type of HMAC keys utilized by the DHCP server to send updates to the DNS server. Rather than making changes to a single record though, zone transfers send the entire zone file, including all records.

How to do it...

1. Generate another HMAC key to use in authenticated zone transfers:

   ```
   dnssec-keygen -a HMAC-SHA512 -b 512 -n HOST -r /dev/urandom
   tsigkey
   ```

2. Create a file called `transfer.key` and insert the following content with `<key>` replaced by the string marked `Key:` in the `.private` file. Copy it to `/etc/bind` on both the master and slave servers:

   ```
   key TRANSFER {
   algorithm HMAC-SHA512;
   secret "<key>";
   };
   ```

3. Include `transfer.key` on both the master and slave servers in `/etc/bind/named.conf.local`:

   ```
   include "/etc/bind/transfer.key";
   ```

4. Modify the zone definition on your master server to send notifications of changes to the slave and allow transfers:

   ```
   zone "example.org" {
   type master;
   notify yes;
   file "/var/lib/bind/example.org.db";
   also-notify { 192.168.1.254; }; // Slave server IP
   allow-transfer { key TRANSFER; };
   allow-update { key DDNS; };
   }
   ```

5. Configure `bind9` on your second server to be a slave for your zone, and tell it to use the `TRANSFER` key for communicating with your master server:

```
zone "example.org" {
type slave;
masters { 192.168.1.1; };
file "/var/lib/bind/example.org.db";
};
server 192.168.1.1 {
keys { TRANSFER; };
};
```

How it works...

Zone transfers use the same HMAC-based communication method (TSIG) that is used for updating zones by the DNS server. In order to implement the least privilege, we do want to use a different key set, though. There is no reason for a slave server to have write access to the master in our use case. Additionally, we may not want the DHCP server to be able to download the complete zone file.

The rest of the configuration has to make do with telling the master to notify the slave in the event of a change and having the slave know how to trigger a transfer as well as serve DNS requests.

3

Configuring IPv6

In this chapter, we will cover configuring IPv6 on your network. Specifically:

- ▸ Setting up an IPv6 tunnel via Hurricane Electric
- ▸ Using ip6tables to firewall your IPv6 traffic
- ▸ Route an IPv6 netblock to your local network

Introduction

The IPv4 protocol used on the Internet today was first deployed on ARPANET in 1983. It uses 32 bit addresses, which limits the number of IP addresses to 4,294,967,296. While this may seem like a lot, that number is being rapidly depleted, even with the boost that NAT provided us.

The replacement, IPv6, improves on IPv4 by switching to 128 bit addressing, which should provide enough IP address space for the foreseeable future. It also makes a number of other improvements including auto-configuration of addresses, simplified processing for routers due to more standardized sizes for packet headers, and additional areas as well.

Even with those improvements, and the impending IPv4 exhaustion, IPv6 has had an extremely slow rollout. The initial design was completed in 1998 but as of the end of 2009 the percentage of users who visited Google with IPv6 connectivity was below 0.25%. Since 2009, adoption has accelerated, with the user saturation increasing from less than 3% to more than 5% in 2014 alone. In mid-2015, the rate was above 8%.

Part of the issue is the incompatibility between the two protocols. You can consider IPv6 a completely separate protocol, which may operate in parallel with IPv4. In order to cope with this reality, networks typically roll it out in a dual stack configuration where systems have IPv4 and IPv6 addresses and provide a preference to one or the other depending on needs.

Depending on your ISP, you may find that you already have a dual protocol network stack enabled. We're going to start off by assuming that this is not already in place, and we will set up IPv6 networks using one of the existing public tunnel providers which provide IPv6 connectivity tunneled over IPv4. You can think of it as being similar to a VPN.

Setting up an IPv6 tunnel via Hurricane Electric

Hurricane Electric is a major backbone and colocation provider based in the US. In addition to their hosting/transit services, they also host http://tunnelbroker.net, another free IPv6 tunnel provider, and `http://ipv6.he.net/certification`, a training and certificate site for learning about IPv6 networking.

Unlike AYIYA tunnels from SixXS, IPv6 tunnels from Hurricane Electric operate over IP protocol 41, which is defined by the IPv6 Encapsulation protocol (RFC2473). This is a separate protocol from ICMP, TCP and UDP.

The downside of this approach is that it does not operate over NAT firewalls natively. This may be an issue if your new firewall device is operating behind an ISP firewall with its own NAT. The ability to forward protocol 41 traffic to a machine behind the NAT is device specific and does not work on all firewalls.

How to do it...

1. Visit `https://tunnelbroker.net` and click **Sign up now!**, and sign up for a Free account.

2. Under **User Functions**, click **Create Regular Tunnel**. You may create up to 5 tunnels.

3. Enter your IP address under **IPv4 endpoint**.

4. Select a tunnel end point which is close to you.

5. Collect the local and remote IPv4 and IPv6 addresses provided by HE's website, and use them to populate your configuration.

6. For Ubuntu/Debian systems, you can then configure the interface in `/etc/network/interfaces`, the code is as follows:

```
auto he-ipv6
iface he-ipv6 inet6 v4tunnel
        address CLIENTIPv6
        netmask 64
        endpoint SERVERIPv4
        local CLIENTIPv4
        ttl 255
        gateway SERVERIPv6
```

7. For configuring on the command line, you can use:

```
modprobe ipv6
ip tunnel add he-ipv6 mode sit remote SERVERIPv4 local LOCALIPV4
ttl 255
ip link set he-ipv6 up
ip addr add LOCALIPv6 dev he-ipv6
ip route add ::/0 dev he-ipv6
ip -f inet6 addr
```

How it works...

Hurricane Electric IPv6 tunnels use the standard 6in4 Tunnel Protocol (RFC4213) that's built automatically into both net-tools (`ifconfig`) and iproute2 (`ip` command). Additionally, Debian and Ubuntu have support for 6in4 built directly into their network initialization scripts, which allow for simplified configuration.

▸ `ip tunnel add he-ipv6 mode sit remote SERVERIPv4 local LOCALIPV4 ttl 255`: This command adds a Simple Internet Transition (SIT) tunnel, which is represented as an interface named he-ipv6. SIT tunnels require that you provide both the local and remote ipv4 addresses.

▸ `ip link set he-ipv6 up`: Bring up our new he-ipv6 interface

▸ `ip addr add LOCALIPv6 dev he-ipv6`: Assign your local ipv6 address to that interface.

Using ip6tables to firewall your IPv6 traffic

Firewalling IPv6 traffic on Linux is handled by the ip6tables command. This tool is the IPv6 version of the `iptables` command we've already used, and it operates in almost exactly the same manner. The big difference is that with IPv6 the use of NAT is highly discouraged.

How to do it...

Let's run the command to establish.

```
# ip6tables -6 -A INPUT -i lo -j ACCEPT
# ip6tables -6 -A INPUT -m state --state ESTABLISHED,RELATED -j ACCEPT
# ip6tables -6 -A INPUT -p tcp --dport 22 -j ACCEPT
# ip6tables -6 -P INPUT DROP
# ip6tables -6 -P FORWARD DROP
# ip6tables -6 -P OUTPUT ACCEPT
# ip6tables -6 -A FORWARD -i eth0 -j ACCEPT
# ip6tables -6 -A FORWARD -i eth1 -o eth0 -m \
state --state RELATED,ESTABLISHED -j ACCEPT
# ip6tables -6 -A FORWARD -i eth0 -j ACCEPT
```

How it works...

The ip6table rules here are identical to the `iptables` rules in *Chapter 1, Configuring a Router* with a few exceptions:

- A lack of NAT
- -6 options

NAT was initially created to deal with the problem of a limited supply of IPv4 addresses. Over time, people began to think of NAT as a security control, which was not its intended purpose. The use of NAT additionally introduces a number of protocol specific problems, and a variety of IP range conflicts when connecting multiple internal networks which may use overlapping RFC1918 address ranges.

With IPv6 we have plenty of IP addresses to be allocated, so the best practice is to instead depend on host and network firewalling as well as secure configuration of services rather than depending on the use of NAT to obscure access to systems.

The -6 option does not do anything in ip6tables. In `iptables` however, the -6 option tells the command to ignore the option. Similarly, there is a -4 option in `iptables` which does not have any effect, but will tell ip6tables to ignore the command.

The beauty of this configuration is that you can then have a single rules file that can be processed by both `iptables` and ip6tables and each command will only take action against the rules that it should pay attention to.

Route an IPv6 netblock to your local network

So far, all we've done is allocate a single IPv6 address to your machine that is hosting the tunnel. One of the nice things about IPv6 however, is the ability to obtain a large number of public IP addresses for your local networks rather than using NAT. In fact, Hurricane Electric and SixXS both offer complementary /48 networks to use with your tunnel. A /48 includes 2^80 IP addresses, or 1,208,925,819,614,629,174,706,176. Much better than the one IPv4 address you typically get from a consumer IP address. To utilize them, you just need to advertise their availability.

How to do it...

Install `radvd` via your package management system:

1. Configure `/etc/radvd.conf`:

```
interface eth1
{
    AdvSendAdvert on;
    prefix 2001:DB8:1:1::/64
    {
    };
};
```

2. Start `radvd` via the `init` script or as appropriate for your distribution.

How it works...

Rather than requiring DHCP for IP address allocation (although DHCPv6 is available if desired), IPv6 implements the **Neighbor Discovery Protocol** (**NDP**) as defined by RFC 2461. NDP uses multicast on the link layer to discover neighbors and routers on the local network and can allow client systems to auto configure addresses for themselves based upon what address ranges local routers are advertising.

The Router Advertisement Daemon, or `radvd`, is an open source implementation of the Neighbor Discovery Protocol. The simple configuration that we provide here advertises the 2001:DB8:1:1::/64 network on eth1. 2001:DB8:1:1::/64 is part of a larger /32 network which is made available for documentation purposes. You should instead replace this value with the /64 network that you obtained from SixXS, Hurricane Electric, or your ISP.

4

Remote Access

In this chapter, we will cover the following points:

- ► Installing OpenSSH
- ► Using OpenSSH as a basic shell client
- ► Using OpenSSH to forward defined ports
- ► Using OpenSSH as a SOCKS proxy
- ► Using OpenVPN

Introduction

One of the nice things about having a Linux network is the ability to access it remotely in a secure manner. Best of all, you have a number of options available to you depending on your needs.

Installing OpenSSH

Our first option for remote access is the simplest, assuming that you just need to be able to remotely access a shell on your Linux system. All Linux distributions offer the ability to install a **Secure Shell** (**SSH**) server. The most common SSH server available is OpenSSH, which is distributed by the OpenBSD team. A lighter weight option called Dropbear is also available and is often found in embedded Linux platforms, such as OpenWRT.

How to do it...

Installing OpenSSH on a Linux system is very easy but the specifics on how to do it will depend on the Linux distribution that you are using.

Let's install SSH server in Debian/Ubuntu through the following command:

```
# sudo apt-get install ssh
```

For Fedora, CentOS, and other RedHat derivatives, it would be `sudo yum install openssh-server`.

Now, once OpenSSH is installed, anyone with network access to tcp port 22 on your system may attempt to log in to your system. If this machine is your firewall or if you forward port 22 from your firewall to this box, it could potentially mean anyone on the Internet. In fact, if this is the case, you can expect to see the attempt to log in to your system using common usernames and passwords within hours of installing the package. There are a few common steps that you should take in order to avoid being the next victim to have their system attempting to brute force the world. The steps are:

- ▶ Use strong passwords. When you first installed your Linux distribution, did you use a trivial password like *password* or any other dictionary words? Or worse, have no password at all? If this is the case, then you can expect to be exploited quickly. This also applies to system accounts that you may have created for a manually installed software package or web service.

- ▶ Restrict who can log in `sshd_config`, which is in `/etc/` or `/etc/ssh/`. The default is to allow logins for all users. On a minimum, you can disable root logins by setting `PermitRootLogin` number. For more control, you can choose to supply a comma separated list of usernames to `AllowUsers` in order to limit logins to just those users.

- ▶ You may choose to additionally move SSH to a non-standard port using the Port definition in `sshd_config`. This option will not provide any protection against a determined attacker, but will at least limit noise from SSH brute force attacks since they're typically performed with a script limited to the default ssh port of 22.

- ▶ Another method to deal with bots is with the using a tool that monitors failed logins and uses firewall rules to block access for repeat offenders. This will limit the scope of their attack attempts to a configurable number of login attempts. A few tools that implement this method are fail2ban and DenyHosts.

- ▶ Finally, for a high value system, you can consider using SSH keys rather than passwords for logins. This allows you to replace fairly weak passwords/passphrases with SSH public keys using RSA, DSA, or ECDSA cryptography, which are not feasible to attack. Note that this would need to be used in conjunction with disabling password authentication in `sshd_config` or it will not provide any additional security.

How it works...

Once installed, OpenSSH listens on TCP port 22 and allows authenticated SSH clients to connect and perform a number of actions including the following:

- ▶ Obtaining a shell (the most common usage)
- ▶ Forwarding defined TCP ports from the client to the server or vice versa, including ports on remote systems.
- ▶ Dynamically forwarding TCP ports by acting as a SOCKS proxy for any application that supports SOCKS4 or SOCKS5.
- ▶ Forwarding X11 applications from the remote system to display on your local system.
- ▶ Copying files using **scp (secure copy)** or **sftp (secure file transfer program)**. Note that sftp is different than ftps, which is the much older FTP protocol operating over SSL.
- ▶ Acting as a layer 2 or layer 3 VPN.

The server provides a public cryptographic key upon login that can be used to validate that the server is what you expect it to be. While there is no public CA infrastructure like you'd have with TLS in order to validate the authenticity of the server, you can either choose to trust the server certificate on first login and inspect for changes to the key or you may share the public key via an external secure channel prior to your login.

For login authentication purposes, the sshd daemon either requires read access to `/etc/passwd` and `/etc/shadow` or more commonly ties into your system's **PAM** (**Pluggable Authentication Modules**) system, which provides a layer of abstraction between services and the actual authentication system under the covers.

As mentioned in the preceding section, you may also choose to use SSH keys, which leverage PAM for user account information but will require the user to have a private key that matches a public key specified in `~/.ssh/authorized_keys`. You can read more about the use of public key cryptography with SSH by running `man ssh-keygen`.

Using OpenSSH as a basic shell client

You have a number of client options if you're looking to access a shell on a system running an SSH daemon.

How to do it...

If you are connecting from another `*nix` system, such as Linux or Mac OS X, you can launch a terminal and use the SSH command-line tool from OpenSSH:

▶ A free graphical SSH client called PuTTY is available for Linux, Mac, and Windows. PuTTY provides you a terminal on the remote system rather than providing any form of local shell access. Windows binaries and the sources to build `*nix` clients can be obtained at `http://www.chiark.greenend.org.uk/~sgtatham/putty/`.

▶ Various SSH clients are also available for Android and iOS devices.

How it works...

The OpenSSH client available on the terminal from systems similar to `*nix` is the simplest approach. Simply launch `Terminal.app` on your Mac or an `xterm` on your Linux system and run `ssh username@host`. If the `username@` is omitted, then the `ssh` client will attempt to log in using your local username. The host may be a valid DNS record or an IP address. You may optionally supply a port with `-p PORT` in the event that you have your SSH daemon running on a non-standard port.

PuTTY, on the other hand, provides a graphical manner to supply the host information:

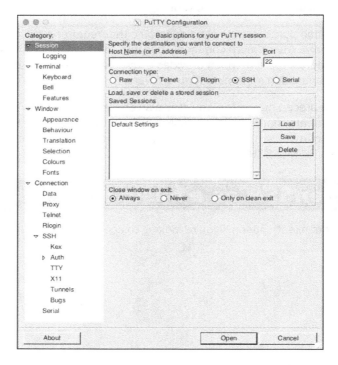

Upon login, you will be prompted for the username and password. Alternatively, the username may be supplied in advance under the **Connection | Data** section of the menu.

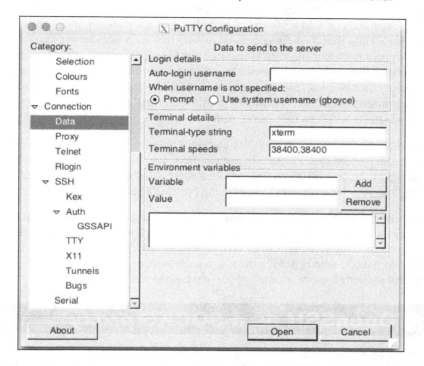

Using OpenSSH to forward defined ports

One extremely useful piece of functionality is the ability to forward ports from the remote system to your local system or vice versa.

How to do it...

- ▶ Forward a remote port locally: `-L 8000:192.168.1.123:80`
- ▶ Forward a local port remotely: `-R 5000:localhost:22`
- ▶ Make either port available from remote systems with `-g`

How it works...

The `-L` option allows you to make a remote port available locally. The arguments are `[bind_address:]port:host:hostport`.

In our example, we're logging into a remote system and then forwarding port 80 on 192.168.1.123 of your local system. This means that if you connect your web browser to localhost port 8000, you will actually be hitting the server on 192.168.1.123. This is useful for accessing resources behind a firewall or just changing the network your connection is established from. Note that if you're specifically using this for a web server, you may need to play tricks with your host files or ports in use in order to work around web applications that expect the correct **Host** header or attempt to redirect your connection to a specific port. You'll also want to note that binding to local ports under 1024 require that you run as root, which is why we've forwarded port 80 to port 8000 locally. If you need to make it available on port 80 instead, you will need to run as root using sudo.

The -R option works the same way with the same arguments, but makes a local network port accessible on the remote side instead. In our example, we're taking localhost port 22 and making it available on port 5000 on the remote system. This would allow users of the remote system to log into your local system by specifying port 5000 to their SSH client.

The default behavior for both of these commands is to bind to a localhost so that only local users may have access to connect to the remote resource. This may be changed with the −g option, which tells the ssh client to bind to all addresses instead, making the forwarded port available to anyone who is able to establish a connection to it. Be sure that you fully understand the security implications of this option before you use it.

Using OpenSSH as a SOCKS proxy

If you're looking to access webpages through an SSH proxy, you may find that the −L option is a bit too limiting, since you need to specify each individual web server that you're forwarding and give each one its own local port.

If your remote network contains an HTTP proxy like Squid or Apache's mod_proxy, then you may choose to forward the port of that proxy server. If you don't have one available, then consider using OpenSSH's built in SOCKS proxy functionality.

How to do it...

Enabling the SOCKS proxy is trivial. Just specify −D 8000 where 8000 is the local port that you want to configure the clients to use. Then just configure your client to use that port as a SOCKS proxy. For some clients, you'll need to explicitly tell them to use remote DNS if you're connecting to resources which are not remotely resolvable.

The following screenshot will show you how to configure this in a modern version of Firefox. The actual configuration of a SOCKS proxy will vary based on the software.

Configure Proxies to Access the Internet

　No proxy

　Auto-detect proxy settings for this network

　Use system proxy settings

◉ Manual proxy configuration:

　　HTTP Proxy: 　　　　　　　　　　　　Port: 　0 ⌄

　　　　　　　Use this proxy server for all protocols

　　SSL Proxy: 　　　　　　　　　　　　　Port: 　0 ⌄

　　FTP Proxy: 　　　　　　　　　　　　　Port: 　0 ⌄

　　SOCKS Host: localhost　　　　　　　Port: 8000 ⌄

　　　　　　　SOCKS v4 ◉ SOCKS v5 ☑ Remote DNS

　No Proxy for:

　localhost, 127.0.0.1

　　Example: .mozilla.org, .net.nz, 192.168.1.0/24

　Automatic proxy configuration URL:

　　　　　　　　　　　　　　　　　　　Reload

　Do not prompt for authentication if password is saved

　?　　　　　　　　　　　　Cancel　　　OK

How it works...

Once you have a port set up as a SOCKS proxy, it listens for valid SOCKS proxy requests. Once received, the SSH client forwards the request on to the SSH daemon, which then establishes a connection to the remote system. The SSH client and daemon then work together to forward the requests and responses back and forth between the client and server.

This functionality can be incredibly useful if you are on an untrusted network and want to be able to browse the internet without concerns about traffic sniffing on the local network.

Using OpenVPN

OpenVPN is a full SSL VPN solution that allows you to connect two networks at layer 2 or 3 via a TCP or UDP tunnel. It is available on `https://openvpn.net/` or via your distributions package repositories.

OpenVPN offers a number of options for authentication. We're going to set up a simple configuration, which will get you up and running. From there, there are multiple options, which you may want to consider for your needs.

How to do it...

1. Install OpenVPN on the server with `sudo apt-get install openvpn` for Debian derivatives like Ubuntu, or `sudo yum install openvpn`.

2. Generate a static key:

    `openvpn --genkey --secret /etc/openvpn/static.key`

3. Set up the server configuration. You can see examples in `/usr/share/doc/ openvpn/examples/sample-config-files`. For our purpose, we'll start with the following:

    ```
    proto udp
    user nobody
    secret /etc/openvpn/static.key
    ifconfig 10.8.0.1 10.8.0.2
    comp-lzo
    verb 3
    ```

4. Create a client configuration file:

    ```
    remote wanaddress
    proto udp
    dev tun
    secret /path/to/static.key
    ifconfig 10.8.0.2 10.8.0.1
    route 192.168.1.0 255.255.255.0
    comp-lzo
    verb 3
    ```

5. Copy the static key to the client via `scp`, copy/paste, or another manner. You'll want to make sure that you keep this key secure as it will now allow access to your network.

6. (Optional) If your OpenVPN server is not the router for your local network, you'll need to forward port 1194 to your `openvpn` server, and define a static route which routes traffic addressed to 10.8.0.2 to your OpenVPN system.

7. Connect the VPN from the client as root:

    ```
    sudo openvpn --config client.conf
    ```

8. You should now be able to ping any IP on your local network.

How it works...

For authentication purposes, OpenVPN offers the ability to use TLS certificates for both the client and server or optionally use a single static key. In this case, we're using the static key approach for a fast and easy configuration. This method requires that we share a single key generated by OpenVPN's `genkey` command on both ends of the connection.

Let's look at the server configuration:

```
proto udp
user nobody
secret /etc/openvpn/static.key
ifconfig 10.8.0.1 10.8.0.2
comp-lzo
verb 3
```

To start with, we're specifying that we'll run over the UDP protocol. OpenVPN supports tunneling over both TCP and UDP, but UDP is recommended and is the default. The reason for this is because UDP does not include any re-transmission functionality. When transmitting TCP or UDP over a tunnel, an additional layer of fault tolerance below it can cause unnecessary overhead in the event of packet loss where both TCP layers attempt to solve the problem.

Next we will specify the user that the `openvpn` daemon should run as. This is a security precaution which makes sure that in the event of a compromise of the daemon, the user will get access to an unprivileged account rather than root.

Next we specify the secret file. You'll want to provide the complete path to where the file may be found. In my example, I've used the `openvpn` configuration directory used on Ubuntu systems.

The `ifconfig` command is used to specify the tunnel end points. The first IP address is the address on the local system that will provide a connection to the second IP, which is the client tunnel endpoint.

`comp-lzo` is an optional configuration option that provides `lzo` compression for the connection. This utilizes more CPU power in order to compress the network traffic, which may substantially increase your throughput in the event that you're sending highly compressible content like text. If your traffic is mostly already encrypted/compressed or binary, you may see less improvement. In this event you may decide to disable the option.

Finally, `verb 3` defines the verbosity level for logging purposes. `Verb 3` is considered medium output and is useful for normal operation. When troubleshooting a problem, you may want to use 9 instead, which is the verbose level.

Ok, now we'll look at the client configuration:

```
remote wanaddress
proto udp
dev tun
secret /path/to/static.key
user nobody
ifconfig 10.8.0.2 10.8.0.1
route 192.168.1.0 255.255.255.0
comp-lzo
verb 3
```

You'll see that the configuration here is very similar. The big differences are that you're specifying a host to connect to via the `remote` variable. This may be the hostname or IP address of your public IP address.

The options to `ifconfig` are also reversed since we're creating the opposite side of the tunnel so the local versus remote variables changed.

We also add a new route variable that will define the IP ranges which are tunneled. Traffic from the client in this case will be routed over the internet as normal unless the recipient traffic is in the 192.168.1.0/24 range, in which case `openvpn` will tunnel the traffic.

Now that the configuration files exists, we can launch the `openvpn` client by running `sudo openvpn --client openvpn.conf`. The `sudo` is required here, as setting up tunnels requires root privileges. Once the daemon is running, it will drop privileges to the user that you specified in the user variable.

5
Web Servers

In this chapter we will cover:

- ► Configuring Apache with TLS
- ► Improving scaling with the Worker MPM
- ► Setting up PHP using an Apache module
- ► Securing your web applications using mod_security
- ► Configuring NGINX with TLS
- ► Setting up PHP in NGINX with FastCGI

Introduction

One of the powerful things that Linux on servers allows you to do is to create scalable web applications with little to no software costs. We're going to discuss setting up web applications on Linux using Apache HTTPD and NGINX (pronounced Engine-X), securing those servers and look at some of the limitations for scaling.

Apache HTTPD, commonly referred to as just Apache, is the number one web server software in the world. As of November 2015, it is estimated to host roughly half of all websites live on the Internet. It was initially created as a set of patches to the NCSA HTTPD server in 1995. In fact, the name Apache was a play on the fact that it was *a patchy server*. These days Apache HTTPD is a very robust, flexible, and feature packed web server option.

NGINX is a newer offering, with the initial release having come out in October of 2004. While less feature filled than Apache, it can often handle a larger load while utilizing less memory than Apache does. It can also be used as a load balancer or reverse proxy frontend for language specific application servers, such as Mongrel from the Ruby on Rails project.

Configuring Apache with TLS

These days, installing Apache with TLS is easier than ever, although the specific process can vary from distribution to distribution due to differences in configuration layout. Let's look at two of the current major examples.

How to do it...

Let's start installing and configuring on Ubuntu 14.04:

1. Install the package:

    ```
    sudo apt-get install apache2
    ```

2. Enable the SSL modules and stock SSL configuration:

    ```
    sudo a2enmod ssl
    ```

    ```
    sudo a2ensite default-ssl
    ```

3. Add the appropriate SSL certs to the machine. The private key file should be delivered to `/etc/ssl/private` while the public certificate and relevant intermediate certs should be delivered to `/etc/ssl/certs`.

4. Update the Apache configuration to point to the correct certs. Edit `/etc/apache2/sites-enabled/default-ssl.conf` in the editor of your choice and update the `SSLCertificateFile` and `SSLCertificateKeyFile` variables to point to your new cert and key. If you're hosting your own internal CA, you'll want to uncomment `SSLCertificateChainFile` and point it to your CA chain.

5. Restart the service:

    ```
    service apache2 restart
    ```

Let's start installing and configuring on CentOS 7:

1. Install apache and `mod_ssl`:

    ```
    sudo yum install httpd mod_ssl
    ```

2. Add the appropriate SSL certs to the machine. The private key file should be delivered to `/etc/pki/tls/private` while the public certificate and relevant intermediate certs should be delivered to `/etc/pki/tls/certs`.

3. Update the Apache configuration to point to the correct certs. Edit `/etc/httpd/conf.d/ssl.conf` in the editor of your choice and update the `SSLCertificateFile` and `SSLCertificateKeyFile` variables to point to your new cert and key. If you're hosting your own internal CA, you'll want to uncomment `SSLCertificateChainFile` and point it to your CA chain.

4. Enable `httpd` to start on boot:

   ```
   sudo systemctl enable httpd.service
   ```

5. Start the daemon:

   ```
   service httpd start
   ```

How it works...

In order to serve SSL/TLS traffic, you need to have Apache installed, as well as a module for Apache which supports the protocol. In this case, we're using `mod_ssl`, which enables OpenSSL support for Apache. Another option would be to use `mod_gnutls`, which uses `GnuTLS`.

In the Ubuntu case, `mod_ssl` is included automatically in the apache2 package. You just need to enable it using a2enmod (Apache 2 Enable Module) and a2enableconf (Apache 2 Enable Configuration). Ubuntu will automatically launch the Apache process on boot up.

For CentOS, you need to install the additional `mod_ssl` package instead, but once installed it is enabled automatically. CentOS does require an additional step in order to enable the daemon on boot up however, which is handled via `systemctl`, part of the system package.

Improving scaling with the Worker MPM

Apache2 offers a variety of **Multi-Processing Modules** (**MPM**) for defining how the daemon will handle scaling. The default is typically prefork, which is a simple MPM which uses separate processes for handling each request. Scaling can be improved by using the Worker MPM or the newer Event MPM, which utilize threading in addition to processes in order to improve performance.

How to do it...

Configuring the worker MPM on Ubuntu 14.04.

Ubuntu 14.04 uses the multi-threaded Event MPM by default, but it may be disabled automatically if any non-threadsafe modules such as `mod_php` are enabled.

To determine which MPM is in use, `execute a2query -M` in order to determine what is configured.

You may then swap out the existing MPM with:

```
a2dismod mpm_$(a2query -M)
a2enmod mpm_worker
service apache2 restart
```

> **Note**:
> That the preceding action will fail if you have any non-thread safe modules enabled.

Configuring the Worker MPM on CentOS 7

CentOS 7 uses the prefork MPM by default since it is the more compatible offering, but it does ship a variety of MPMs in the package. The definition of which MPM is to be used can be found in `/etc/httpd/conf.modules.d/00-mpm.conf`. Just comment out the existing MPM and uncomment the desired one before restarting with `service httpd restart`.

How it works...

In order for Apache to scale to handle large numbers of simultaneous connections, it uses a potentially large number of processes. Each process that runs uses up a fixed amount of memory, meaning that the more connections you are using at a given time, the more memory you are consuming on your system.

Loaded modules such as `mod_php` add to the memory utilization for each process, increasing memory consumption further. Additionally, if your web application code interacts with databases, then each Apache process that is running code which interacts with the database will require its own database connection. This can cause additional resource strains as you increase the number of connections that your database needs to deal with.

In order to give people the flexibility for how they handle connections, Apache is very configurable. There are directives which define the number of processes to run at startup (`StartServers`), as well as a minimum and maximum number of spare/idle servers which should be running (`MinSpareServers`, `MaxSpareServers`).

For workloads that require the ability to handle many more connections, you need to look into Apache's options for **Multi-Processing Modules** (**MPM**). The two main MPMs you should look at for Unix-like systems are the pre-fork MPM, which is the default, and the worker MPM.

The pre-fork MPM allows for a single connection per process. So if you want to be able to handle 500 simultaneous connections, then you'll need to start 500 processes, utilizing 500 times the resources of a single process.

The worker MPM is a hybrid approach that uses a combination of processes and threads to increase capacity without increasing memory utilization as much. This MPM module adds an additional directive called `ThreadsPerChild` that defines the number of threads each process will run. With a default of 25 threads, this means that you can handle 500 connections using just 20 processes, thus dramatically decreasing your required memory.

The event MPM is similar to worker, but attempts to handle request processing more cleanly by handing off connections which are idle but being kept open by a browser to separate threads which can easily just sit and wait until additional processes are brought in.

Now, there is a very good reason why the pre-fork MPM is the default rather than worker or event. Any code which executes within the Apache webserver, like mod_php, will be running multi-threaded with multi-threaded MPMs. If a module is not thread safe, then you may experience crashes or other problems.

Setting up PHP using an Apache module

PHP is a very common programming language to use on Apache webserver, largely due to its ease of use. Luckily this also equates to being very easy to install on most distributions as well.

How to do it...

Setting up PHP on Ubuntu 14.04:

1. Install PHP's apache module:

    ```
    sudo apt-get install libapache2-mod-php5
    ```

2. Ubuntu's package should enable the module by default, but you can test it to be sure by running a2query -m php5. If it is not enabled, it may be enabled by running a2enmod php5.

Setting up PHP on CentOS 7:

1. Install PHP, including the Apache module.

    ```
    sudo yum install php
    ```

2. CentOS also enables the module by default. In order to confirm that it is installed, look for /etc/httpd/conf.modules.d/10-php.conf. If you have difficulties executing PHP code, you may need to restart the Apache service with service httpd restart.

How it works...

The PHP module gets linked into the Apache application during startup, adding the capability to detect PHP web application code and process it automatically. This loading is handled dynamically based upon the webserver configuration file.

Securing your web applications using mod_security

Now that you're able to execute the PHP code, you're also ready for people to attempt to exploit your PHP code. While PHP code can certainly be secure, it often appeals to new developers who have not yet learned secure coding practices. In a situation like this, it can be helpful to have some additional protection in the form of a Web Application Firewall.

Mod_Security is an open source **Web Application Firewall** (**WAF**) for Apache. It is able to interpret full HTTP requests and responses in order to detect and block attempts at performing various HTTP attacks like SQL injection, cross site scripting and others.

How to do it...

The first thing you need to do is to install and enable the module in detection mode:

Installing on Ubuntu 14.04:

1. Install the package:

   ```
   sudo apt-get install libapache2-mod-security2
   ```

2. Setup the mod_security configuration file:

   ```
   sudo cp /etc/modsecurity/modsecurity.conf-recommended /etc/
   modsecurity/modsecurity.conf
   ```

3. Restart the service:

   ```
   Sudo service apache2 restart
   ```

Installing on CentOS 7:

1. Install the package:

   ```
   sudo yum install mod_security
   ```

2. Setup the mod_security core rules set:

   ```
   sudo yum install mod_security_crs
   ```

3. Switch the configuration to detection only:

   ```
   sudo sed -i 's/SecRuleEngine On/SecRuleEngine DetectionOnly/g' /
   etc/httpd/conf.d/mod_security.conf
   ```

4. Restart the service:

   ```
   sudo service httpd restart
   ```

Once it is installed in detection mode, you should start seeing possible exploitation attempts in `/var/log/apache2/modsec_audit.log` on Ubuntu or `/var/log/httpd/modsec_audit.log` on CentOS. You'll want to evaluate any detection exploitation attempts in order to confirm that there are no false positives with your application before enabling it in blocking mode.

Once you're comfortable that the rules are behaving as expected, they can be switched to blocking mode by setting `SecRuleEngine` to on in `/etc/modsecurity/modsecurity.conf` (Ubuntu) or `/etc/httpd/conf.d/mod_security.conf` (CentOS).

How it works...

`Mod_security` works by watching incoming HTTP requests and outgoing HTTP responses and looking for specific patterns that indicate known malicious request types. By default, it is configured with their **Core Rules Set** (**CRS**), but additional rules may be written with a bit of knowledge of the format of the rules. For now, sticking with the core rules or other rules written by experienced users is your best bet.

Rules are defined on the system in `/usr/share/modsecurity-crs/` on Ubuntu or `/usr/lib/modsecurity.d/` for CentOS.

Configuring NGINX with TLS

While we've covered Apache's HTTPD server so far in this chapter, there are other options available for use on Linux platforms as well. One popular offering is NGINX (pronounced engine-x), which works well as a lightweight, fast, multithreaded offering.

We're going to look at how to set it up as a TLS webserver.

How to do it...

Installing on Ubuntu 14.04:

1. Install the software:

   ```
   sudo apt-get install nginx
   ```

2. Configure the server for TLS by uncommenting the HTTPS server section of `/etc/nginx/sites-available/default` while populating the `ssl_certificate`, `ssl_certificate_key` and `ssl_ciphers` variables.

3. Restart the daemon:

   ```
   sudo service nginx restart
   ```

Installing on CentOS 7:

1. On CentOS 7, NGINX is not included in the default repos, but is available in the **Extra Packages for Enterprise Linux** (**EPEL**) repository.

2. Install the EPEL repo:

   ```
   sudo yum install epel-release
   ```

3. Install the nginx package:

   ```
   yum install nginx
   ```

4. Configure the server for TLS by adding an https server section to /etc/nginx/nginx.conf:

   ```
   server {
       listen          443 ssl;
       server_name     localhost;

       ssl_certificate        /etc/pki/tls/certs/certw.crt;
       ssl_certificate_key    /etc/pki/tls/private/cert.key;

       ssl_session_cache      shared:SSL:1m;
       ssl_session_timeout    5m;

       ssl_ciphers    HIGH:!aNULL:!MD5;
       ssl_prefer_server_ciphers    on;

       location / {
           root    html;
           index    index.html index.htm;
       }
   }
   ```

5. Enable nginx to start on boot:

   ```
   systemctl enable nginx
   ```

6. Restart nginx:

   ```
   Service nginx restart
   ```

How it works...

For the most part, the configuration of NGINX is very straightforward. The only complicated part is the enabling of the EPEL repository on CentOS systems. This is required as nginx is not supported by Red Hat as a part of the core Red Hat Enterprise distribution, which CentOS is part of.

Setting up PHP in NGINX with FastCGI

As we mentioned is an earlier chapter, linking modules into a multi-threaded HTTP server requires that the code in the module be thread safe. NGINX works around this by utilizing the `fastcgi` protocol to interact with interpreters rather than linking them directly into the process. This does not have quite the performance of the more native approach, but you can limit what content runs through the processor.

How to do it...

Configuring on Ubuntu 14.04:

1. Install the PHP FastCGI wrapper:

   ```
   sudo apt-get install php5-fpm
   ```

2. Modify php's configuration file to disable `cgi.fix_pathinfo`, this setting opens the door to security vulnerabilities by allowing PHP to *guess* at what your request was intending to request:

   ```
   sed 's/.*cgi.fix_pathinfo=.*/cgi.fix_pathinfo=0/g' /etc/php5/fpm/php.ini
   service php5-fpm restart
   ```

3. Configure `nginx` to talk to the php5-fpm daemon (default is `/etc/nginx/sites-available/default`) within the relevant server definitions:

   ```
   location ~ \.php$ {
     try_files $uri =404;
     fastcgi_pass unix:/var/run/php5-fpm.sock;
     fastcgi_index index.php;
     fastcgi_param SCRIPT_FILENAME \
   $document_root$fastcgi_script_name;
     include fastcgi_params;
   }
   ```

4. Restart `nginx`:

   ```
   service nginx restart
   ```

Configuring on CentOS 7:

1. Install the PHP FastCGI wrapper:

    ```
    sudo apt-get install php-fpm
    ```

2. Enable the `php` wrapper to start on boot:

    ```
    systemctl enable php-fpm
    ```

3. Modify PHP's configuration file to disable `cgi.fix_pathinfo`, this setting opens the door to security vulnerabilities by allowing PHP to *guess* at what your request was intending to request:

    ```
    sed 's/.*cgi.fix_pathinfo=.*/cgi.fix_pathinfo=0/g' /etc /php.ini
    service php-fpm restart
    ```

4. Configure `nginx` to talk to the `php-fpm` daemon (default is `/etc/nginx/nginx.conf`) within the relevant server definitions:

    ```
    location ~ \.php$ {
        root            html;
        fastcgi_pass    127.0.0.1:9000;
        fastcgi_index   index.php;
        fastcgi_param   SCRIPT_FILENAME \
          $document_root/$fastcgi_script_name;
        include         fastcgi_params;
    }
    ```

5. Restart `nginx`:

    ```
    service nginx restart
    ```

How it works...

The `php5-fpm`/`php-fpm` packages on Ubuntu/CentOS install a daemon which listens on a Unix socket or TCP port and accepts PHP code for processing. This allows us to handle the PHP code without having the `php` library linked into the web server but without requiring the overhead of starting a CGI application for each request.

Now that we have a service which handles PHP interpretation, `nginx` can concentrate on serving up normal HTML, JavaScript and image content and can essentially proxy any PHP requests directly to php5-fpm directly. It then passes the responses back to `nginx` for the server to serve up to users.

The same approach may be leveraged on Apache boxes as well, which should allow you to use a multi-threaded MPM and still process PHP without worrying about threading issues in the interpreter.

6
Directory Services

In this chapter, we will cover:

- ▶ Configuring Samba as an Active Directory compatible directory service
- ▶ Joining a Linux box to the domain

Introduction

If you have worked in corporate environments, then you are probably familiar with a directory service such as Active Directory. What you may not realize is that Samba, originally created to be an open source implementation of Windows file sharing (SMB/CIFS), can now operate as an Active Directory compatible directory service. It can even act as a **Backup Domain Controller** (**BDC**) in an Active Directory domain. In this chapter, we will configure Samba to centralize authentication for your network services. We will also configure a Linux client to leverage it for authentication and set up a RADIUS server, which uses the directory server for authentication.

Configuring Samba as an Active Directory compatible directory service

As of Samba 4.0, Samba has the ability to act as a **primary domain controller** (**PDC**) in a manner that is compatible with Active Directory.

How to do it...

Installing on Ubuntu 14.04:

1. Configure your system with a static IP address and update `/etc/hosts` to point to that IP address rather than localhost.

2. Make sure that your time is kept up to date by installing an NTP client:

   ```
   sudo apt-get install ntp
   ```

3. Pre-emptively disable `smbd`/`nmbd` from running automatically:

   ```
   sudo bash -c 'echo "manual" > /etc/init/nmbd.override'
   sudo bash -c 'echo "manual" > /etc/init/smbd.override'
   ```

4. Install Samba and `smbclient`:

   ```
   sudo apt-get install samba smbclient
   ```

5. Remove stock `smb.conf`:

   ```
   sudo rm /etc/samba/smb.conf
   ```

6. Provision the domain:

   ```
   sudo samba-tool domain provision --realm ad.example.org --domain
   example --use-rfc2307 --option="interfaces=lo eth1" --option="bind
   interfaces only=yes" --dns-backend BIND9_DLZ
   ```

7. Save the randomly generated admin password.

8. Symlink the AD krb5.conf to `/etc`:

   ```
   sudo ln -sf /var/lib/samba/private/krb5.conf /etc/krb5.conf
   ```

9. Edit `/etc/bind/named.conf.local` to allow Samba to publish data:

   ```
   dlz "AD DNS Zone" {
       # For BIND 9.9.0
       database "dlopen /usr/lib/x86_64-linux-gnu/samba/bind9/dlz_
   bind9_9.so";
   };
   ```

10. Edit `/etc/bind/named.conf.options` to use the Kerberos `keytab` within the options stanza:

    ```
    tkey-gssapi-keytab "/var/lib/samba/private/dns.keytab";
    ```

11. Modify your zone record to allow updates from Samba:

    ```
    zone "example.org" {
      type master;
      notify no;
      file "/var/lib/bind/example.org.db";
    ```

```
    update-policy {
        grant AD.EXAMPLE.ORG ms-self * A AAAA;
        grant Administrator@AD.EXAMPLE.ORG wildcard * A AAAA SRV
CNAME;
        grant SERVER$@ad.EXAMPLE.ORG wildcard * A AAAA SRV CNAME;
        grant DDNS wildcard * A AAAA SRV CNAME;
    };
};
```

12. Modify `/etc/apparmor.d/usr.sbin.named` to allow bind9 access to a few additional resources within the `/usr/sbin/named` stanza:

```
/var/lib/samba/private/dns/** rw,
/var/lib/samba/private/named.conf r,
/var/lib/samba/private/named.conf.update r,
/var/lib/samba/private/dns.keytab rk,
/var/lib/samba/private/krb5.conf r,
/var/tmp/* rw,
/dev/urandom rw,
```

13. Reload the `apparmor` configuration:

    sudo service apparmor restart

14. Restart `bind9`:

    sudo service bind9 restart

15. Restart the Samba service:

    sudo service samba-ad-dc restart

Installing on CentOS 7:

Unfortunately, setting up a domain controller on CentOS 7 is not possible using the default packages provided by the distribution. This is due to Samba utilizing the Heimdal implementation of Kerberos while Red Hat, CentOS, and Fedora using the MIT Kerberos 5 implementation.

How it works...

The process for provisioning Samba to act as an Active Directory compatible domain is deceptively easy given all that is happening on the backend. Let us look at some of the expectations and see how we are going to meet them as well as what is happening behind the scenes.

Active Directory requirements

Successfully running an Active Directory Forest has a number of requirements that need to be in place:

▶ **Synchronized time**: AD uses Kerberos for authentication, which can be very sensitive to time skews. In our case, we are going to use `ntpd`, but other options including `openntpd` or `chrony` are also available.

▶ **The ability to manage DNS records**: AD automatically generates a number of DNS records, including SRV records that tell clients of the domain how to locate the domain controller itself.

▶ **A static IP address**: Due to a number of pieces of the AD functionality being very dependent on the specific IP address of your domain controller, it is recommended that you use a static IP address. A static DHCP lease may work as long as you are certain the IP address will not change. A rogue DHCP server on the network, for example, may cause difficulties.

Selecting a realm and domain name

The Samba team has published some very useful information regarding the proper naming of your realm and your domain along with a link to Microsoft's best practices on the subject. It may be found on: `https://wiki.samba.org/index.php/Active_Directory_Naming_FAQ`.

The short version is that your domain should be globally unique while the realm should be unique within the layer 2 broadcast domain of your network.

Preferably, the domain should be a subdomain of a registered domain owned by you. This ensures that you can buy SSL certificates if necessary and you will not experience conflicts with outside resources.

`Samba-tool` will default to using the first part of the domain you specified as the realm, ad from ad.example.org. The Samba group instead recommends using the second part, example in our case, as it is more likely to be locally unique.

Using a subdomain of your purchased domain rather than a domain itself makes life easier when splitting internal DNS records, which are managed by your AD instance from the more publicly accessible external names.

Using Samba-tool

Samba-tool can work in an automated fashion with command line options, or it can operate in interactive mode. We are going to specify the options that we want to use on the command line:

```
sudo samba-tool domain provision --realm ad.example.org --domain example
--use-rfc2307 --option="interfaces=lo eth1" --option="bind interfaces
only=yes" --dns-backend BIND9_DLZ
```

The realm and domain options here specify the name for your domain as described above.

Since we are going to be supporting Linux systems, we are going to want the AD schema to support RFC2307 settings, which allow definitions for UID, GID, shell, home directory, and other settings, which Unix systems will require.

The pair of options specified on our command-line is used for restricting what interfaces Samba will bind to. While not strictly required, it is a good practice to keep your Samba services bound to the internal interfaces.

Finally, Samba wants to be able to manage your DNS in order to add systems to the zone automatically. This is handled by a variety of available DNS backends. These include:

- ▶ `SAMBA_INTERNAL`: This is a built-in method where a Samba process acts as a DNS service. This is a good quick option for small networks.

- ▶ `BIND9_DLZ`: This option allows you to tie your local named/bind9 instance in with your Samba server. It introduces a named plugin for bind versions 9.8.x/9.9.x to support reading host information directly out of the Samba data stores.

- ▶ `BIND_FLATFILE`: This option is largely deprecated in favor of BIND9_DLZ, but it is still an option if you are running an older version of Bind. It causes the Samba services to write out zone files periodically, which Bind may use.

Bind configuration

Now that Samba is set up to support `BIND9_DLZ`, we need to configure named to leverage it. There are a few pieces to this support:

- ▶ `tkey-gssapi-keytab`: This setting in your named options section defines the Kerberos key tab file to use for DNS updates. This allows the Samba server to communicate with the Bind server in order to let it know about zone file changes.

- ▶ `dlz setting`: This tells Bind to load the dynamic module, which Samba provides, in order to have it read from Samba's data files.

- ▶ `Zone updating`: In order to be able to update the zone file, you need to switch from an allow-update definition to update-policy, which allows more complex definitions including Kerberos based updates.

- ▶ `Apparmor rules changes`: Ubuntu uses a Linux Security Module called **Apparmor**, which allows you to define the allowed actions of a particular executable. Apparmor contains rules restricting the access rights of the named process, but these existing rules do not account for integration with Samba. We need to adjust the existing rules to allow named to access some additional required `resources`.

Joining a Linux box to the domain

In order to participate in an AD style domain, you must have the machine joined to the domain using Administrator credentials. This will create the machine's account within the database, and provide credentials to the system for querying the ldap server.

How to do it...

1. Install `Samba`, `heimdal-clients`, and `winbind`:

   ```
   sudo apt-get install winbind
   ```

2. Populate `/etc/samba/smb.conf`:

   ```
   [global]
        workgroup = EXAMPLE
        realm = ad.example.org
        security = ads
        idmap uid = 10000-20000
        idmap gid = 10000-20000
        winbind enum users = yes
        winbind enum groups = yes
        template homedir = /home/%U
        template shell = /bin/bash
        winbind use default domain = yes
   ```

3. Join the system to the domain:

   ```
   sudo net ads join -U Administrator
   ```

4. Configure the system to use `winbind` for account information in `/etc/nsswitch.conf`:

   ```
   passwd:          compat winbind
   group:           compat winbind
   ```

How it works...

Joining a Linux box to an AD domain, you need to utilize winbind that provides a PAM interface for interacting with Windows RPC calls for user authentication. Winbind requires that you set up your `smb.conf` file, and then join the domain before it functions. `Nsswitch.conf` controls how `glibc` attempts to look up particular types of information. In our case, we are modifying them to talk to `winbind` for user and group information.

Most of the actual logic is in the `smb.conf` file itself, so let us look:

1. Define the AD Domain we're working with, including both the workgroup/domain and the realm:

    ```
    workgroup = EXAMPLE
    realm = ad.example.org
    ```

2. Now we tell Samba to use **Active Directory Services** (**ADS**) security mode:

    ```
    security = ads
    ```

3. AD domains use **Windows Security IDs** (**SID**) for providing unique user and group identifiers. In order to be compatible with Linux systems, we need to map those SIDs to UIDs and GIDs. Since we're only dealing with a single client for now, we're going to let the local Samba instance map the SIDs to UIDs and GIDs from a range which we provide:

    ```
    idmap uid = 10000-20000
    idmap gid = 10000-20000
    ```

4. Some Unix utilities such as finger depend on the ability to loop through all of the user/group instances. On a large AD domain this can be far too many entries so Winbind suppresses this capability by default. For now, we're going to want to enable it:

    ```
    winbind enum users = yes
    winbind enum groups = yes
    ```

5. Unless you go through specific steps to populate your AD domain with per-user home directory and shell information, then Winbind will use templates for home directories and shells. We'll want to define these templates in order to avoid the defaults of /home/%D/%U (/home/EXAMPLE/user) and /bin/false:

    ```
    template homedir = /home/%U
    template shell = /bin/bash
    ```

6. The default `winbind` configuration takes users in the form of `username@example.org` rather than the more Unix style of user username. Let's override that setting:

    ```
    winbind use default domain = yes
    ```

7

Setting up File Storage

In this chapter, we are going to cover:

- ► Serving files with SMB/CIFS through Samba
- ► Granting authenticated access
- ► Setting up an NFS server
- ► Configuring WebDAV through Apache

Introduction

Once you have a network with multiple devices, it is useful to be able to share files easily between them and between users. Building a centralized file server achieves this goal as well as provides a central point for backing up your data. In this chapter, we will explore several available protocols for storing files. We will start with the SMB/CIFS protocols, commonly used by Windows systems, and work our way to services specifically designed for synchronizing mobile clients.

Serving files with SMB/CIFS through Samba

We are going to start by setting up a simple read-only file server using Samba, and then we will expand on it from there. If you are not familiar with SMB/CIFS, you may know it by another name, Windows File Sharing. This is the protocol, which Microsoft uses for its built-in file sharing, but re-implemented by the Samba project.

How to do it...

1. Install Samba:

   ```
   sudo apt-get install samba
   ```

2. Edit /etc/samba/smb.conf:

   ```
   [global]
      server role = standalone server
      map to guest = Bad User
      syslog = 0
      log file = /var/log/samba/log.%m
      max log size = 1000
      dns proxy = No
      usershare allow guests = Yes
      panic action = /usr/share/samba/panic-action %d
      idmap config * : backend = tdb
   [myshare]
      path = /home/share
      guest ok = yes
      read only = yes
   ```

3. Restart smbd:

   ```
   sudo service smbd restart
   ```

4. You should now be able to browse the share like you used to do in Windows file share.

How it works...

The Global section of the above configuration is a slimmed-down version of the Ubuntu default Samba configuration. The specifics of our configuration live in the [share] definition.

The [share] defines the name of the file share. You could instead choose to call it [files] or most any other name you would like to use. At a minimum, the name *global* is reserved and cannot be used for a share.

path: This defines the path that you're looking to share out.

guest ok: This defines if a password is required to access the service or not. If guest ok = yes, then unauthenticated guest logins are allowed. There is also an option for *guest only*, which disallows password login if it's set to yes.

The read-only option defines if users should be able to write to the share or not. It defaults to *no*, but if set to *yes* then you are only allowed to read the share's content, not change it in any way.

Granting authenticated access

Samba supports granting authenticated access to shares in addition to making them available as public shares.

How to do it...

1. Select the account that you want to use for authentication. All Samba share accounts must be accompanied by a Unix account. In this case, we'll user a new user called `testuser`:

   `sudo useradd testuser`

2. Create a separate Samba-specific password for that account:

   `sudo smbpasswd -a testuser`

3. Modify `smb.conf` to set the valid users for the share:

   ```
   [myshare]
     path = /home/share
     guest ok = yes
     read only = yes
      valid users = testuser
   ```

4. Access the share once again; confirming that this time, you are prompted for a username and password.

How it works...

As mentioned in the preceding, Samba users must be backed by a system user account that is known to PAM. This could mean a user in `/etc/passwd`, or it could mean a user account coming from some sort of directory service. In this case, we are going to create a dedicated user account.

Authentication however is handled separately from the password defined in `/etc/shadow`. You need to have a Samba-specific password, which might be defined by `smbpasswd`.

Finally, you use the *valid users* definition to restrict access to the share.

Setting up an NFS server

NFS, or Network File System, was initially created by Sun Microsystems to allow clients to access remote file shares on Unix systems back in the 80s. NFS is trivial to set up and is typically rather fast, but it can introduce some interesting security issues if it is not done correctly.

How to do it...

1. Install NFS server:

    ```
    sudo apt-get install nfs-kernel-server
    ```

2. Configure shares within /etc/exports:

    ```
    /directory/to/share client(options)
    ```

3. Install the NFS client software:

    ```
    sudo apt-get install nfs-common
    ```

4. Mount the share:

    ```
    mount -t nfs4 server:/directory/to/share /mountpoint
    ```

How it works...

The nice thing about NFS is how trivial it is to set up. You simply install the NFS server, configure /etc/exports and go. The only real details to learn and understand are some of the options available and their implications:

> ▶ **Path to share**: This is the absolute path to the directory on the server, which you want to export. For ease of maintenance, it is recommended that you add a level of indirection using symlinks to repoint the path. For example, instead of exporting / home, export /exports/home and have /exports/home be a symlink to /home. This will allow you to repoint to new locations on the disk in the future if you so desire.

> ▶ **Client definition**: This is how we define what systems may mount the share. You can define it via an IP address, hostname, or a NIS Netgroup if you are using NIS on your network. Hostnames or IP addresses may be specified with a wildcard if desired (192.168.1.* or *.domain.com) or you can specify IP addresses by CIDR block or with a netblock (192.168.1.0/24 or 192.168.1.0/255.255.255.0). Note that hostname lookups are done via reverse DNS records (PTR records), so you must have them set up properly in order for it to work.

> ▶ Finally options, of which there are a lot available. Here are a few major ones to keep in mind:

>> ❏ ro/rw: This determines if the share will be read only or read/write. Shares are read only by default unless rw is added as an option.

>> ❏ sync/async: NFS shares are synchronous by default, meaning that when a write operation is performed on a file, the NFS server will not reply to the client until that write has been written to the disk. This behavior ensures a more consistent state in the event of a server crash, but has performance implications, especially on slow media. You may use the async option in order to make writes asynchronous instead.

□ root_squash/no_root_squash: Root Squash is a security control that tells the server to map requests from the root (uid 0) user to the *nobody* user in order to prevent a malicious client from being able to perform actions on the server with superuser privileges. It is the default behavior but it can be overridden with no_root_squash.

The client side also has a number of mount options available, which can be specified with a -o to the mount command or in options specified in /etc/fstab. The client has even more options available than the server, but we will just look at some of the common ones again.

▶ hard/soft: Hard versus soft mounts determine what should happen in the event that your connection to the NFS server is lost. Soft mounts will report an error in that case while a hard mount will instead block until the file server returns.

▶ nosuid: Don't allow setuid binaries on NFS.

▶ tcp/udp: Access the NFS server over the TCP (the default) or UDP. TCP has a small performance hit in certain use cases due to the overhead of the TCP protocol, but it performs better on heavily congested networks. In the event that the connection to the server is dropped due to a connection problem, TCP will revert to attempting to establish a connection, issuing SYN requests with a back off, while a UDP mount will continue to attempt to send data to the server since it does not know the connection is dead.

There's more...

Unlike many other file services, most NFS servers do not provide any sort of strong authentication/authorization. Instead, NFS exposes standard Unix file permissions and file ownership via UIDs. The client system is responsible for enforcing access control at that point. This means that it is possible for a malicious client to access any files or directories it would like to, regardless of file ownership.

The biggest examples of this problem are the UID collisions. Let us say that you have a file server that contains /home/alice, which is owned by Alice's account with UID 1000. /home is exported via NFS and made available to other client systems on the network. Now let's say that Bob owns a desktop machine which uses UID 1000 for his user account as well. If Bob mounts /home from the NFS share, his system will show that /home/alice and all of its contents are owned by Bob, and will grant access to all of the files.

A common solution to the collision problem is to have all client systems of the NFS share a centralized directory service such as NIS or LDAP. This will protect you against accidental collisions from trusted client systems but not from malicious systems.

The newer solution that should protect against malicious clients as well is the use of Kerberized NFS. This refers to protecting your NFS share with a Kerberos system such as MIT's Kerberos 5 implementation or a system like Active Directory.

Configuring WebDAV through Apache

WebDAV was initially created as a protocol for managing web server content over http/https. In other words, it grants you the ability to add, remove, or edit HTML and support web content remotely.

From there, the usage expanded to provide access to general file services as well. For example, Apple's iDisk service (part of `iTools/.Mac/MobileMe`) supported accessing your files through any WebDAV client. This support unfortunately ended when iDisk was retired with the transition to iCloud.

WebDAV clients are built into Mac OS X and Windows as well as the file managers for Gnome, KDE and many other Linux desktop environments. You can even find Linux console tools, which support the protocol or mount it directly on your filesystem using the `davfs2` filesystem driver.

How to do it...

We are going to start by assuming that you already have Apache running. If you do not, then please read the chapter on Apache configuration prior to starting. You will also want to ensure that you have SSL/TLS configured on your webserver, since WebDAV requires you to authenticate and you do not want to send credentials in the clear.

1. Install some extra required Apache modules:
   ```
   sudo apt-get install libapache2-mod-authnz-external
   sudo apt-get install libapache2-mod-authz-unixgroup
   ```

2. Enable the `dav` and `dav_fs` Apache modules:
   ```
   sudo a2enmod dav
   sudo a2enmod dav_fs
   sudo a2enmod authnz-external
   sudo a2enmod authz-unixgroup
   sudo service apache2 restart
   ```

3. Create a new site configuration for the path that you want to share in `/etc/apache2/sites-available/webdav.conf`:
   ```
   <Directory /home/user/test>
           AllowOverride None
           Require all granted
   </Directory>

   <IfModule mod_authnz_external.c>
           AddExternalAuth pwauth /usr/sbin/pwauth
   ```

```
            SetExternalAuthMethod pwauth pipe
    </IfModule>

    Alias "/test" "/home/user/test/"
    <Location "/test/">
            Dav on
            AuthType Basic
            AuthName "Restricted Files"
            AuthBasicProvider external
            AuthExternal pwauth
            require unix-group groupname
            Order allow,deny
            Allow from all
            Options Indexes
    </Location>
```

4. Enable the new site:

    sudo a2ensite webdav

    sudo service apache2 reload

5. Grant write access to the Apache process:

    sudo chgrp www-data /home/user/test

How it works...

There are a few things at play here, so we are going to tackle them one at a time.

Apache modules

First, we enable the dav and dav_fs Apache modules. The dav module provides Apache with the information on how to speak the WebDAV protocol. The dav_fs module provides Apache with the information on how to translate the WebDAV requests into filesystem operations. This allows you to actually interface with your local filesystems.

The reason dav and dav_fs are separate is because it is possible to utilize additional DAV providers that interface with other systems instead of your local filesystem. One common example is the dav_svn module, which allows you to interface with a Subversion version control system over the WebDAV protocol.

Next, we enable authnz-external. The authnz-external module supports mod_auth_basic in authenticating users. The auth_basic module handles HTTP Basic Auth between the web browser and the web server. The authnz-external provider assists Apache in actually validating the user's password once it has been provided. Like all authnz modules, it provides Authentication (represented by the N) and Authorization (represented by the Z). In this case, it handles these through an external application which we must define.

Finally, we enable `authz_unixgroup`, which provides Authorization (there is that Z again) based upon looking up the user within a defined user group on the system, defined in `/etc/groups`.

Directory directive

The default Ubuntu Apache configuration in `/etc/apache2/apache2.conf` includes a `Directory` directive for `/` that denies access for all users:

```
<Directory />
        Options FollowSymLinks
        AllowOverride None
        Require all denied
</Directory>
```

Access to specific directories, such as the `webroot` are then explicitly granted via more specific `Directory` directives:

```
<Directory /var/www/>
        Options Indexes FollowSymLinks
        AllowOverride None
        Require all granted
</Directory>
```

In our example, we want to serve traffic from space in `/home/user`, so we need to make sure that there is a matching `Directory` directive to grant access to that path. We do it in the above configuration using:

```
<Directory /home/user/test>
        AllowOverride None
        Require all granted
</Directory>
```

On versions of Linux where SELinux or other **Mandatory Access Control** (**MAC**) systems are in place, additional steps may be required to grant access via the MAC system as well.

Authnz_external configuration

Next, we configure the `authnx_external` module in order to ensure that it knows what external tool to use for validating the user supplied username and passwords:

```
<IfModule mod_authnz_external.c>
        AddExternalAuth pwauth /usr/sbin/pwauth
        SetExternalAuthMethod pwauth pipe
</IfModule>
```

Here we tell the module to use `pwauth` for testing the credentials. This tool is a simple `setuid` binary, which is installed as a dependency for libapache2-mod-authnz-external. It accepts a username and password via standard in (STDIN) and then issues a return code of `0` for success or any other return code for failure. `AddExternalAuth` defines available methods while `SetExternalAuthMethod` tells Apache how to interact with the method. In this case, we are going to use a Unix pipe.

Directory definition

Now we define the actual rules for accessing the new directory. Here is where we actually enable authentication and authorization as well as enabling WebDAV:

```
Alias "/test" "/home/user/test/"
<Location "/test/">
        Dav on
        AuthType Basic
        AuthName "Restricted Files"
        AuthBasicProvider external
        AuthExternal pwauth
        require unix-group groupname
        Order allow,deny
        Allow from all
        Options Indexes
</Location>
```

Most of this is straightforward Apache configuration. Aliases map web server directories to filesystem directories (`http://server/test` pulls content from `/home/user/test`), while the location directive defines the rules for accessing content from `/test`.

The configuration directives within the location section break down into a few basic groups:

Authentication/Authorization:

▶ **AuthType Basic**: Enables HTTP Basic Auth for this directory.

▶ **AuthName Restricted Files**: Defines the Realm for HTTP basic authentication, as defined in RFC 1945.

▶ **AuthBasicProvider external**: Defines the authentication provider that `mod_auth_basic` should use to validate passwords.

▶ **AuthExternal pwauth**: This defines the External Auth provider that we want to use, as defined by our `AddExternalAuth` statement.

▶ **require unix-group groupname**: Configures the unix group which authenticated users must be a member of in order for them to be granted access to the directory. It configures the `authz_unixgroup` Apache module. You could instead use `require user username1, username2` or `require valid-user`, which would then utilize `authnz_external` instead.

Basic Apache directory configuration:

▶ Order allow, deny / allow from all: Should we utilize a default deny or default allow? These directives are commonly used to configure host based access control. Do you want to restrict access by hostname or IP address? We're not doing so in this case, but you could instead choose to use *Order deny, allow* and then only allow from specific IP address ranges, or perhaps keep allow, deny but block certain known bad IPs.

▶ Options Indexes: If you do not have an existing index file such as `index.html`, should a directory listing be provided instead?

Enable WebDAV:

Dav on: The *Dav* directive defines if WebDAV should be enabled or not. It defaults to Off, but can also take the WebDAV provider name as an argument as well. *On* exists as an alias to the *filesystem* provider which `dav_fs` provides for us.

Granting write access

At this point, we have provided WebDAV access to the directory space, but you may find that any attempts to actually change the content of that space fail. This is because even though you have authentication to Apache as your own user, Apache is actually operating as the unprivileged www-data user. If we want write operations to succeed, then Apache will need to have write access to that space.

There are a few ways in which we can handle this:

▶ Make `/home/user/test` world writable (not recommended)

```
chmod -R 777 /home/user/test
```

▶ Change ownership of the directory and its files to www-data:

```
chown -R www-data /home/user/test
```

▶ Change group ownership of the directory and its files to www-data and make them group readable/writable:

```
chgrp -R www-data /home/user/test
chmod g+rw /home/user/test
```

▶ Add www-data to an existing group with the appropriate permissions:

```
sudo usermod -a -G existingroup www-data
```

The method to use will depend a lot on your use case but, in general, you should use the method, which limits your exposure as much as possible. You want to make sure that you do not grant access to your files beyond the users who need it and you need to make sure that you do not grant more access to the web server process than you need to.

8

Setting up E-mail

In this chapter, we will cover:

- ▸ Configuring Postfix to send and receive e-mail
- ▸ Setting up DNS records for e-mail delivery
- ▸ Configuring IMAP
- ▸ Configuring authentication for outbound e-mail
- ▸ Configuring Postfix to support TLS
- ▸ Blocking spam with Greylisting
- ▸ Filtering spam with SpamAssassin

Introduction

E-mail, specifically the **Simple Mail Transport Protocol** (**SMTP**), is one of the oldest protocols on the Internet. Even after all this time, it is still heavily utilized by most businesses out there. While these days hosted e-mail infrastructure like hosted Exchange or Google apps is quite common, but it's still a good idea to understand what is occurring under the cover. In this chapter, you'll set up your own e-mail infrastructure, which is able to send and receive mail over the public internet. We'll also learn some basic methods for dealing with the problem of unsolicited commercial e-mail (spam).

There are a few core pieces to e-mail infrastructure:

- ▸ **Mail Transfer Agent** (**MTA**): The MTA is responsible for receiving an e-mail message from the network or from local processes, determining if it should be accepted or rejected, and then pass it either on to the next MTA or hand off the message to an MDA for delivery. A few common examples of MTAs for Linux are Sendmail, Postfix, or Exim.

▶ **Mail Delivery Agent** (**MDA**): The MDA is responsible for taking an e-mail message from the MTA, and delivering to local mailboxes, potentially running through rule logic first. A few common MDAs are /bin/mail (the Sendmail MDA) and procmail.

▶ **Mail User Agent** (**MUA**): This is your mail client like Thunderbird, Mutt, Pine, and so on. It may read your e-mail from local mail spools on your system, or it may interact with a remote mail server via a protocol like POP3 or IMAP.

In this chapter, we're going to work on setting up an SMTP server to handle inbound and outbound e-mail and an IMAP server to handle making the mail available to your e-mail client. We'll also look at some of the capabilities that a Unix mail server gives you, such as complex mail filtering using procmail.

Configuring Postfix to send and receive e-mail

The most important part of any e-mail system is the MTA. This system is responsible for handling delivery of e-mail messages, both outbound and inbound. It can also be the downfall of your mail system if it is improperly configured, which could result in your system being used for sending SPAM mail to other destinations.

One of the original and most well known MTAs is Sendmail, which dates back to 1983. It is a very powerful tool, and unfortunately very easy to get wrong. In fact, the configuration language for Sendmail is so obtuse that there is actually a macro language called m4, which is commonly used for generating Sendmail configurations. M4 makes configuring Sendmail much simpler, but there are other options available which natively use a sane configuration language like Postfix.

The great thing about Postfix as opposed to a number of other SMTP servers is that it is built with a set of sane, safe defaults. Additionally, any setting, which is not defined within your configuration file uses that default. This allows for very stripped down configuration files, although you are certainly free to define all the defaults within your configuration file if you want. In fact, Postfix makes that easy to do as well with the include of the postconf tool.

How to do it...

1. Install postfix and the supporting mailutils package:

   ```
   sudo apt-get install postfix mailutils
   ```

2. Create the postfix configuration at /etc/postfix/main.cf containing:

   ```
   mydomain = domain.com
   mydestination = $mydomain $myhostname
   mynetworks = 127.0.0.0/8
   ```

3. Restart the postfix service:

```
postfix reload
```

How it works...

The great thing about Postfix as opposed to a number of other SMTP servers is that it is built with a set of sane, safe defaults. Additionally, any setting, which is not defined within your configuration file uses that default. This allows for very stripped-down configuration files, although you are certainly free to define all the defaults within your configuration file if you want. In fact, Postfix makes that easy to do as well with the inclusion of the `postconf` tool.

The `postconf` tool is a simple mechanism for interacting with your Postfix server configuration. If you run `postconf` on its own, it will dump out all configuration options and their current value. You could choose to redirect this output to your main.cf file in order to specify the values for all available configuration options explicitly. While not likely to occur, this could potentially protect you against the default value changing after an update in a way which you were not expecting.

You may also choose to run `postconf` with a specific variable name in order to limit output to just that one variable. `postconf -d` can be used in order to print out the default value of a setting rather than the one configured on your specific system. You may also use `postconf -e` in order to edit the settings in `/etc/postfix/main.cf`. This can be helpful for scripting set up of Postfix.

There are three specific items that we chose to override in the preceding configuration:

▶   **mydomain**: The default value for `mydomain` on recent versions of Postfix is `localdomain`. We want to change this to be our local domain. In a default Postfix configuration the `mydomain` variable gets referenced either directly or indirectly by a number of other configuration parameters.

▶   **mydestination**: This variable defines what hostnames we accept mail for. The default behavior is to accept e-mail for `$myhostname`, localhost `$mydomain` and localhost. For our purpose, we're going to restrict that to just `$mydomain` and `$myhostname`. You can choose to add additional hostnames you want to accept mail for if you have multiple domains.

▶   **mynetworks**: This defines a list of networks which you trust for relaying mail. Any IP address or CIDR block defined in here can just blindly send mail through us. The default includes 127.0.0.0/8 (localhost) and all subnets that your machine is directly part of, which is potentially a bit too wide open for our needs.

There's more...

There are a few things you should know if you're going to operate your own mail server. RFC2142 defines a number of mail addresses that all internet sites should accept e-mail for and should be reviewed:

▶ **Postmaster**: E-mail addressed to `postmaster@domain` should be accepted by your mail system and should go to someone relevant. This address can be used by people operating other mail servers when they detect a problem with your e-mail system (open relays, mail flooding, and so on).

▶ **Abuse**: E-mail should be accepted for `abuse@domain` and also to allow people to report perceived abuse of your system. This is typically, where spamming complaints will end up. This is very useful in the rare case where you accidentally turn your mail system into an open relay, deploy a web application, which can be used to send e-mails without proper restrictions, or if a user of your system is just not behaving.

▶ **Hostmaster**: Issues with your DNS infrastructure will be typically sent to hostmaster.

▶ **Webmaster/www**: These are used to report issues with web servers.

There are others as well, but these are the ones for the most commonly used services.

Setting up aliases

No one is going to want to set up e-mail accounts for each of the above addresses. While it is doable, it may result in the messages being reviewed less frequently than they should be. An alternative is to set up mail aliases. Aliases are e-mail addresses that just forward messages to another defined email address.

Mail aliases are defined within `/etc/aliases` and are of the format of **aliasaddress: destinationaddress**. The destination may be the local part of another user account, or it could be a fully qualified e-mail address. For example, you may choose to point abuse to the root user with an alias of **abuse: root**. One common approach is to point host master, postmaster and abuse to the root user, and then optionally forward the root user to your own account on the box or on a remote e-mail system.

To add aliases, just edit `/etc/aliases` to make your change and then run the `newaliases` command.

Setting up a smarthost

When broadband internet was first starting to be deployed within the US, one common thing that a new Linux user would do would be to create and run their own mail system. This typically just required setting up software like Postfix, and properly configuring it to send and receive e-mail.

These days things are a bit trickier. In an effort to curtail spamming, more and more broadband providers are starting to block outbound port 25 traffic from user networks which do not go through mail relays that the ISP owns and operates. This has made a significant reduction in spam, but it does make operating your own mail server more difficult.

Often the only step you need to take is to set up a smart host. A smart host is a mail server that acts as a relay for other servers. Your machine may be able to send its own outbound e-mail as long as it forwards the messages on to your ISP's smart host for delivery rather than trying to deliver the messages itself. IP ranges may restrict this smart host, or it could be set up to require authentication.

Relays without authentication

To set up Postfix to use a smart host without authentication, simply set the `relayhost` variable to `[ispserver]`. For a example, you could set `relayhost = [smtp.domain.com]`.

The purpose of the `[]` characters around the hostname is to tell Postfix to not look up MX records and instead use the CNAME/A records. It does not matter in this case, but in some cases, it may mean the difference between sending messages to the correct relay host and sending messages to a machine that may reject the mail.

If you need to specify a non-standard port, add:**PORT** after the brackets. For example: `[smtp.domain.com]:587`

Relays with Auth

If your smarthost requires you to log in with your username and password, then that can be done by enabling SASL auth, and specifying a SASL password map.

```
relayhost = [smtp.gmail.com]:587
smtp_sasl_auth_enable = yes
smtp_sasl_password_maps = hash:/etc/postfix/relay_password
smtp_sasl_security_options = noanonymous
default_destination_concurrency_limit = 4
soft_bounce = yes
smtp_tls_security_level = may
```

The above example uses a Gmail account for outbound mail delivery. `/etc/postfix/relay_password` should contain:

```
smtp.gmail.com user@gmail.com:password
```

Due to the sensitivity of the data, make sure to `chmod 600` the file. You must then run `postmap /etc/postfix/relay_password`, which will then create the Berkeley DB file which Postfix actually reads.

Setting up DNS records for e-mail delivery

When configuring a properly set up mail server, there are a number of DNS records you need to set up in order to ensure that the system functions as expected. Some of these are defined in RFC974, which covers mail routing and the DNS system.

The main piece you need to understand is **Mail Exchanger** (**MX**) records. These records define how e-mail destined to a given domain should be handled. Without an MX record being defined, e-mail addressed to `user@domain.com` would be sent to the domain.com A record, which is often an HTTP server. For some smaller sites, this may be reasonable if their HTTP server is also an SMTP server, but that is not always the case.

Rather than depending on the A record, you can instead use one or more MX records with defined priorities that point to A records which may be in or out of the domain you're configuring. For example, your e-mail could go to smtp.domain.com. Alternatively, if Google Apps handles your e-mail, you may have multiple MX records within the Google.com domain instead.

How to do it...

Assuming you've already gone through the process of setting up your DNS infrastructure, or you're at least using your DNS registrar's infrastructure, then setting up the MX records themselves is pretty straightforward. The format of the records is:

```
DOMAIN TTL IN MX PRIORITY MAILSERVER
```

As a shortcut, you can use @ as an alias for the zone you're using. For example, in the `domain.com` zone file, @ would symbolize domain.com. You may also choose to create MX records for subdomains, for example `test.domain.com`, which would then be able to receive its own e-mail to a separate server. Here are some examples of what those MX records may look like:

```
@ 600 IN MX 10 smtp.domain.com.
@ 600 IN MX 20 backup.domain.com.
test 600 IN MX 10 test.domain.com.
```

You'll need to make sure that each of the targets of the MX records have matching A records (or CNAMEs). For example:

```
smtp 600 IN A 192.168.1.1
backup 600 IN A 192.168.1.2
test 600 IN A 192.168.1.3
```

How it works...

For a good example, you can look at the MX records for `www.google.com`:

```
$ dig  -t mx google.com

; <<>> DiG 9.8.3-P1 <<>> -t mx google.com
;; global options: +cmd
;; Got answer:
;; ->>HEADER<<- opcode: QUERY, status: NOERROR, id: 58348
;; flags: qr rd ra; QUERY: 1, ANSWER: 5, AUTHORITY: 0, ADDITIONAL: 2

;; QUESTION SECTION:
;google.com.          IN   MX

;; ANSWER SECTION:
google.com.     600   IN   MX   50 alt4.aspmx.l.google.com.
google.com.     600   IN   MX   20 alt1.aspmx.l.google.com.
google.com.     600   IN   MX   30 alt2.aspmx.l.google.com.
google.com.     600   IN   MX   10 aspmx.l.google.com.
google.com.     600   IN   MX   40 alt3.aspmx.l.google.com.

;; ADDITIONAL SECTION:
alt1.aspmx.l.google.com. 274   IN   A   74.125.141.27
alt2.aspmx.l.google.com. 109   IN   A   64.233.186.26

;; Query time: 43 msec
;; SERVER: 192.168.1.1#53(192.168.1.1)
;; WHEN: Fri Jan 29 20:51:02 2016
;; MSG SIZE   rcvd: 168
```

In this example, you can see that e-mail destined for the google.com domain can go to one of 5 hostnames specified in the MX records. The priority field right before the hostname defines what order they will be tried in, from lowest to highest. Multiple records at the same priority would essentially be tried round robin.

Configuring IMAP

Now that you're able to get e-mail delivered, you can read e-mail from the local mail spool by using the mail command. In general, it is more useful to be able to retrieve your e-mail from off the box however, which typically means webmail, pop3 or IMAP. In this recipe, we're going to look at setting up a Dovecot e-mail server.

How to do it...

1. Install the `dovecot-imap` package:

    ```
    sudo apt-get install dovecot-imap
    ```

2. Configure the SSL cert and key:

    ```
    sed 's|^ssl_cert .*|ssl_cert = </path/to/cert|g' /etc/dovecot/
    conf.d/10-ssl.conf
    ```

    ```
    sed 's|^ssl_key .*|ssl_key = </path/to/key|g' /etc/dovecot/
    conf.d/10-ssl.conf
    ```

3. Configure the mail server to require TLS by editing `/etc/dovecot/conf.d/10-master.conf` and set `port = 0` under `inet_listener imap`.

4. Restart the service:

    ```
    service dovecot restart
    ```

How it works...

Ubuntu provides a number of different packages for Dovecot, which provide a number of different services like IMAP, pop3 and manage sieve (simplified e-mail filtering).

Ubuntu ships these with a sane set of defaults, which largely handle a lot of the configuration that we would have had to do. The configuration is split into multiple files, which are then included by the main `/etc/dovecot/dovecot.conf`. The split configuration files are provided in `/etc/dovecot/conf.d` and are a mix of numbered files which end in `.conf` (like `10-ssl.conf`) and files like `auth-passwdfile.conf.ext` which are included from `10-auth.conf`.

The pre-selected configuration automatically authenticates from the local system, and automatically enables TLS with a self-signed certificate. The commands that we run above swap out the self-signed cert for a publicly signed cert that you specify the path to.

Additionally, we want to disable non-TLS IMAP in order to avoid having clients sending their credentials in plaintext. You could also choose to disable plaintext auth for IMAP if it's not under TLS, but that method is not compatible with the PAM authentication that we're going to be using.

Configuring authentication for outbound e-mail

With our current mail server setup, we can retrieve e-mail remotely and we can send mail from the local box, but we cannot send mail from remote systems. In order to enable this functionality, we need to configure Postfix to require auth for sending outbound mail from remote users. Typically, this requires setting up a SASL server of some variety like Cyrus `saslauthd`. In our case, we're going to use Dovecot's built in SASL server.

How to do it...

1. Configure Dovecot to expose its SASL interface to Postfix by editing `/etc/dovecot/conf.d/10-master.conf`:

```
service auth {
...
  unix_listener /var/spool/postfix/private/auth {
    group = postfix
    mode = 0660
    user = postfix
  }
...
}
```

2. Configure Postfix to authenticate via SASL by editing `master.cf` and adding:

```
submission inet n - n - - smtpd
  -o smtpd_tls_security_level=encrypt
  -o smtpd_sasl_auth_enable=yes
  -o smtpd_sasl_type=dovecot
  -o smtpd_sasl_path=private/auth
  -o smtpd_sasl_security_options=noanonymous
  -o smtpd_sasl_local_domain=$myhostname
  -o smtpd_client_restrictions=permit_sasl_authenticated,reject
  -o smtpd_recipient_restrictions=reject_non_fqdn_
recipient,reject_unknown_recipient_domain,reject
```

3. Restart the service:

Service postfix restart

How it works...

Authentication for SMTP works by exposing a SASL interface for Postfix to use, and configuring it to talk via that interface. In our case, we have Dovecot expose its authentication via the Unix socket located in `/var/spool/postfix/private/auth` which is restricted to the Postfix user.

Next we configure the submission port in `master.cf` of Postfix. *Submission* is a secondary SMTP port which typically has authentication forced and is set aside for user interaction rather than server-to-server passing of messages. This allows you to require authentication for the port that users use, and allows you to implement port 25 filtering on non-mail server machines without impacting the user's ability to talk to their e-mail provider.

We set a number of options for the submission port, including:

- ▶ **smtpd_tls_security_level**: This setting defines the TLS requirements for the submission port. We're going to set it to *encrypt*, which forces the use of STARTTLS. You may also chose to set it to *may*, which makes STARTTLS optional.

- ▶ **smtpd_sasl_auth_enable**: Do we want to enable SASL authentication? For our uses we do.

- ▶ **smtpd_sasl_type**: Which flavor of SASL do we want to use? This is going to be Cyrus or Dovecot.

- ▶ **smtpd_sasl_path:** The path to the Unix socket for the SASL service. This may be fully qualified or relative to `$data_directory` (`/var/lib/postfix`).

- ▶ **smtpd_sasl_security_options**: Set security options for the SASL service. In our case, we're disabling anonymous logins in order to prevent the service from being an open relay.

- ▶ **smtpd_client_restrictions**: Rules for allowing messages. We permit the SASL-authenticated users and then deny everyone else.

- ▶ **smtpd_recipient_restrictions**: Rules for which recipient addresses may be e-mailed. We disallow e-mail addresses that aren't fully qualified (`reject_non_fqdn_recipient`) and e-mails addressed to domains, which do not resolve or have an invalid MX record (`reject_unknown_recipient_domain`).

Configuring Postfix to support TLS

Postfix can utilize TLS for securing communication in a few ways. We're going to look at each of them.

How to do it...

1. Require TLS for authentication of local clients:

   This is already handled in our existing configuration through the `smtpd_tls_security_level=encrypt` option for the submission port.

2. Allow TLS of inbound/outbound mail delivery:

   ```
   $ sudo postconf -e smtpd_tls_security_level=may
   ```

3. Set the TLS key and certificate files:

   ```
   $ sudo postconf -e smtpd_tls_cert_file=/path/to/server.crt
   $ sudo postconf -e smtpd_tls_key_file=/path/to/server.key
   ```

How it works...

The most important thing we want to do here is ensure that passwords are not sent in plaintext. This means requiring authentication on the submission port, which the user interacts with.

Unfortunately, when it comes to SMTP delivery, large swaths of the internet still do not allow SMTP over TLS, so forcing TLS may very well result in undeliverable e-mail. Instead we use the `may` keyword to tell Postfix to use TLS if it can, but still allow delivery if it cannot. This is largely reasonable due to the lack of any real authentication in server-to-server SMTP traffic.

Blocking spam with Greylisting

As anyone who has been on the internet for a while knows, e-mail has a big problem with **Unsolicited Commercial E-mail** (**UCE**), also known colloquially as spam. Most of this problem boils down to the fact that the SMTP protocol does not do any validation message senders. While properly configured mail servers will validate their users prior to allowing them to send e-mail from their account, the protocol itself does not prevent random machines on the internet from sending mail from arbitrary users and domains. This allows spammers to send forged e-mails through misconfigured mail systems or simply send the messages themselves directly to the recipient mail server from VMs at hosting providers as well as compromised desktops and servers.

Luckily, there are steps that can be taken in order to detect or limit the spam directed to your system. A few common approaches are:

- **Reputation Block Lists** (**RBLs**) which provide mechanisms for looking up the likelihood that the sender is a spammer based upon past behavior or characteristics of the system. For example, some block lists consider end user IP ranges to be likely spammers since legitimate mail tends to come through the ISP's mail servers while significant amounts of spam come from compromised Windows desktops. The Spamhaus project is one of the better-known RBL providers.

- **Bayesian Filtering**, which uses analysis of the content of both spam and legitimate e-mails in order to determine a statistical likelihood that the message is spam.

- **Greylisting leverages** temporary message rejections in order to limit spam intake. Greylisting primarily protects against spammers who use scripts to send mass quantities of e-mail directly to your mail server. These scripts do not tend to queue and retry delivery of messages, which encounter a non-fatal error from the mail server, while legitimate mail servers do.

Let's start by looking at how we would implement greylisting on our existing Postfix mail server.

How to do it...

1. Install `postgrey`

   ```
   $ sudo apt-get install postgrey
   ```

2. Configure Postfix to use Postgrey as a `check_policy_service`:

   ```
   $ sudo postconf -e smtpd_recipient_restrictions="check_policy_
   service inet:127.0.0.1:10023, permit"
   ```

3. Reload Postfix's configuration:

   ```
   $ sudo postfix reload
   ```

How it works...

Postgrey integrates with Postfix by setting it as a `check_policy_service` within the `smtpd_recipient_restrictions` section of the configuration. When Postfix receives an SMTP connection providing a message recipient via a RCPT TO command, it will pass the collected information about the connection to the `check_policy_service` in order to decide if the message should be accepted or rejected.

Postgrey takes that information and creates a tuple of the mail server IP address, the provided sender e-mail address and the recipient e-mail address. This tuple is looked up in a local Berkeley DB file containing those three fields as well as timestamps for the connection.

The first time a given tuple is seen, the message will be temporarily rejected (as opposed to a failure). Attempts to deliver will continue to be rejected until 5 minutes have passed, after which the message will be successfully delivered. Once the message is accepted, it will be accepted immediately within the next 35 days.

Spammers tend not to retry after the initial attempt, so each recipient it attempts to deliver to will be given the temporary failure and you will never see them again. Legitimate mail servers should retry, so the messages will be delivered. Do note that some badly configured mail servers may not retry for a long period, so you may find that some e-mail arrives much later than it should have the first time you receive a message from that sender.

For domains which you know do not deal well with `greylisting`, you can choose to whitelist sending domains in `/etc/postgrey/whitelist_clients` or whitelist specific destination addresses in `/etc/postgrey/whitelist_recipients`. The default copy of `whitelist_recipients` for Ubuntu includes `postmaster@` and `abuse@`, which is a good practice in order to allow people to report problems with your configuration.

Filtering spam with SpamAssassin

SpamAssassin is a very popular tool, which uses a number of methodologies to identify spam messages and then either filter, tag or drop them. A few of the methods it uses includes Bayesian detection and the use of RBLs.

SpamAssassin can be configured globally by integrating directly with your mail server, or can be implemented on a per client basis through Procmail or integration with your mail client. Thunderbird from the Mozilla project, for example, integrates with SpamAssassin.

How to do it...

Let's look at how to integrate `SpamAssassin` directly in with Postfix.

1. Install `SpamAssassin`:

   ```
   $ sudo apt-get install spamassassin
   ```

2. Enable the running of `spamd`:

   ```
   $ sudo sed -i 's/^ENABLED=.*/ENABLED=1/g' /etc/default/
   spamassassin
   ```

3. Start `spamd`:

   ```
   sudo service spamassassin start
   ```

4. Copy `SpamAssassin`'s example filtering script to a more useful location:

   ```
   $ sudo cp /usr/share/doc/spamassassin/examples/filter.sh /usr/
   local/bin/spamfilter
   ```

5. Modify /etc/postfix/master.cf to add a content filter to the smtp rule at the beginning of the file:

```
smtp   inet n  -  -  -  -  smtpd -o content_filter=spamfilter
```

6. Add a definition for spamfilter at the bottom of /etc/postfix/master.cf:

```
spamfilter
       unix  -  n  n  -  -  pipe
     flags=Rq user=spamd argv=/usr/local/bin/spamfilter \
     -oi -f ${sender} ${recipient}
```

7. Restart postfix:

```
$ sudo postfix reload
```

How it works...

SpamAssassin itself works by using a combination of a daemon called spamd and a client called spamc. The spamc client receives e-mail messages via standard input and passes it to the spamd daemon for processing.

The filter script, which we put into place, accepts e-mail messages from STDIN, passes them through spamc for processing purposes, and then redelivers the processed message back to the mailer daemon via the sendmail binary. The processed messages will be flagged with a header that indicates it is likely spam, which may then be used for filtering in procmail or your mail client.

9
Configuring XMPP

In this chapter we will cover:

- ▶ Installing ejabberd
- ▶ Configuring DNS for XMPP
- ▶ Configuring the Pidgin client

Introduction

The Extensible Messaging and Presence Protocol (XMPP) is a widely implemented open protocol for passing XML messages. It was initially created as an instant messaging platform, but it has since been used by TiVo for communication between their set-top devices and their online scheduler, implemented by Google as Google Talk (since replaced by the non-XMPP Hangouts) and as an interface for Facebook's chat.

In this chapter, we'll learn to set up the ejabberd IM platform for use as your own IM service. We'll leverage XMPP's server-to-server federation to be able to exchange messages with other public XMPP systems and secure the traffic with TLS.

Installing ejabberd

Currently there are a number of Open Source XMPP/Jabber server projects available with their own individual strengths and weaknesses. For this chapter, we're going to look at ejabberd, which is an extremely powerful and flexible option that has great online documentation. The code for ejabberd is written in Erlang, which is a language created for writing distributed, fault tolerant code. While we will not be taking advantage of the native clustering of ejabberd, it does exist for future expansion.

How to do it...

1. Install ejabberd through the following command:

   ```
   sudo apt-get install ejabberd
   ```

2. Restrict access to the authentication script:

   ```
   sudo chown root:ejabberd /usr/lib/ejabberd/priv/bin/epam
   sudo chmod 4750 /usr/lib/ejabberd/priv/bin/epam
   ```

3. Set up the PAM configuration:

   ```
   cat <<< '#%PAM-1.0
   auth        sufficient  pam_unix.so likeauth nullok nodelay
   account     sufficient  pam_unix.so' > /etc/pam.d/ejabberd
   ```

4. Set up /etc/ejabberd/ejabberd.cfg:

   ```
   {loglevel, 3}.

   {hosts, ["example.com"]}.

   %% Use Pam auth
   {auth_method, pam}.
   {pam_service, "ejabberd"}.

   {listen,
    [

     {5222, ejabberd_c2s, [

                        {certfile,
    "/etc/ejabberd/ejabberd.pem"},
    starttls_required,
                        {access, c2s},
                        {shaper, c2s_shaper},
                        {max_stanza_size, 65536}
                       ]},

     {5269, ejabberd_s2s_in, [
                           {shaper, s2s_shaper},
                           {max_stanza_size, 131072}
                          ]},
     {5280, ejabberd_http, [
                         captcha,
                         http_bind,
                         http_poll,
                         web_admin
                        ]}
   ```

```
]}.

%% Traffic Shapers
{shaper, normal, {maxrate, 1000}}.
{shaper, fast, {maxrate, 50000}}.
{max_fsm_queue, 1000}.

%% Traffic Shaping
{access, s2s_shaper, [{fast, all}]}.
{access, c2s_shaper, [{none, admin},
                      {normal, all}]}.

%% Access Limits
{access, max_user_sessions, [{10, all}]}.
{access, max_user_offline_messages, [{5000, admin},
{100, all}]}.
{access, local, [{allow, local}]}.
{access, c2s, [{deny, blocked},
               {allow, all}]}.

{access, announce, [{allow, admin}]}.
{access, configure, [{allow, admin}]}.
{acl, admin, {user, "admin", "example.com"}}.

%% Multi-User Chat Settings
{access, muc_admin, [{allow, admin}]}.
{access, muc_create, [{allow, local}]}.
{access, muc, [{allow, all}]}.

{access, pubsub_createnode, [{allow, local}]}.

{language, "en"}.

%% Modules
{modules,
 [
  {mod_adhoc,    []},
  {mod_announce, [{access, announce}]},
  {mod_blocking,[]},
  {mod_caps,     []},
  {mod_configure,[]},
  {mod_disco,    []},
  {mod_http_bind, []},
  {mod_last,     []},
```

```
        {mod_muc,          [
                             {host, "conference.@HOST@"},
                             {access, muc},
                             {access_create, muc_create},
                             {access_persistent, muc_create},
                             {access_admin, muc_admin}
                           ]},
        {mod_offline,      [{access_max_user_messages,
                             max_user_offline_messages}]},
        {mod_ping,         []},
        {mod_privacy,      []},
        {mod_private,      []},
        {mod_pubsub,       [
                             {access_createnode, pubsub_createnode},
                             {ignore_pep_from_offline, true},
                             {last_item_cache, false},
                             {plugins, ["flat", "hometree", "pep"]}
                           ]},
        {mod_roster,       []},
        {mod_shared_roster,[]},
        {mod_stats,        []},
        {mod_time,         []},
        {mod_vcard,        []},
        {mod_version,      []}
      ]}.
```

5. Restart service:

```
Service ejabberd restart
```

How it works...

The Ubuntu package for ejabberd provides a reasonable start for a configuration which is well commented and provides some reasonable defaults. Rather than attempt to massage their configuration to meet our needs, we create a new configuration from scratch.

While we will be discussing the options which we are configuring, you may find it helpful to also read through the stock configuration in order to learn about some of the additional options that ejabberd can provide for you.

Configuring authentication

Ejabberd has the ability to tie into multiple authentication sources, including its own built-in user management service leveraging its local database. In our case, we're going to tie ejabberd into our existing system accounts by leveraging the service's PAM authentication options.

In order to leverage PAM, there are a few steps that we need to take. The first is to restrict access to the epam helper script that actually performs the authentication attempts. This script is located in /var/lib/ejabberd/priv/bin/epam in the stock source-based install, but it has been moved to /usr/lib/ejabberd/priv/bin/epam instead in Ubuntu. We need to make sure it is setuid and restricted to just the root user and the ejabberd group.

The next step is to make sure that we have a PAM configuration for the ejabberd service by populating /etc/pam.d/ejabberd. We have included an example PAM configuration, but you can write more complex rules for PAM as well.

Finally, we tell ejabberd itself in ejabberd.cfg to use PAM authentication by setting:

```
%% Use Pam auth
{auth_method, pam}.
{pam_service, "ejabberd"}.
```

Configuring listening ports

The configuration also has a section labeled *listen*, which defines the network ports the ejabberd service should listen on. The three services that we have listed have unique uses. You can choose the services you'd like to enable, based upon your use case.

C2S service

This section defines the C2S, or client to server, service. This is the network port that allows users to connect to your XMPP service. You'll need to make sure that this port is accessible from outside of your network if you want to be able to connect while you're remote:

```
{5222, ejabberd_c2s, [
`
  "/etc/ejabberd/ejabberd.pem"},
starttls_required,
{access, c2s},
{shaper, c2s_shaper},
{max_stanza_size, 65536}
]},
```

We've configured the service to require starttls and using the TLS cert and key stored in /etc/ejabberd/ejabberd.pem. One item of note here is that ejabberd requires that your key, cert, and intermediates all be stored within the same file rather than split into separate files.

The configuration also states {access, c2s}, which means that the C2S access control method should be applied to the service. That access control method is defined as:

```
{access, c2s, [{deny, blocked},
               {allow, all}]}.
```

This access control segment directs us to deny access to anyone who is on the admin maintained block list and allow access to everyone else.

Similarly, {shaper, c2s_shaper} directs to use the c2s_shaper rule, which is defined as:

```
{access, c2s_shaper, [{none, admin},
                      {normal, all}]}.
```

This rule allows admin users to send traffic at an unlimited rate, while restricting users to the "normal" rate, which is defined as 1000 bytes per second:

```
{shaper, normal, {maxrate, 1000}}.
```

And finally, we define the max_stanza_size, which is the maximum size in bytes of an XML stanza sent by the client. This simply limits the size of the messages that you're allowed to send.

S2S service

S2S uses a dialback method for communication, meaning that your server connects to the remote server's S2S service on port 5269, which in turn triggers the remote server to connect to port 5269 on your system. The usage of two distinct TCP connections for sending and receiving messages provides additional protections against message spoofing by requiring that both sides initiate their own connection to the published DNS record for the other services:

```
{5269, ejabberd_s2s_in, [
    {shaper, s2s_shaper},
    {max_stanza_size, 131072}
]},
```

Here we define the S2S, or Server to Server inbound message service. This service handles receiving messages from other XMPP domains. It allows users on your server to communicate with users of a different XMPP server.

The configuration for the S2S inbound service is a lot simpler since, there's no real user settings of any sort. There's just a shaper defined and a larger max_stanza_size. The shaper in use for the S2S service is the s2s_shaper that maps to the "fast" shaper with a rate of 50000 bytes per second:

```
{shaper, fast, {maxrate, 50000}}.
```

The reason for the faster limit here is that it keeps track of all server to server communication. This means a higher overhead per message as well as the potential for multiple people communicating if the two servers are popular and have a number of people talking to each other.

Port 5269 for the S2S server will definitely need to be accessible externally. If you do not allow the port to be accessed externally, no server to server messages will function.

HTTP Service

Port 5280 contains the HTTP service, which provides a number of pieces of functionality:

- ▶ `http_bind`: This enables the HTTP bind functionality defined by XEP-0206 - XMPP over BOSH.

- ▶ `http_poll`: This enables the HTTP Polling interfaces defined by XEP-0025: Jabber HTTP Polling.

- ▶ `Web_admin`: This service opens up a web-based admin service for your local admin users.

    ```
    {5280, ejabberd_http, [
            http_bind,
            http_poll,
            web_admin
    ]}
    ```

With the exception of the Web admin interface, the HTTP server component of ejabberd is used as a method to access the XMPP service over the HTTP protocol rather than serving content like a traditional web server. Specifically, it implements APIs that may be used by fully web-based XMPP clients.

Opening port 5280 to the world is optional, based upon if you want to leverage any of the preceding features from outside of your network.

Access control

The biggest item to look at in the access control section is the definition of the admin user. Here is where we define one or more users to be site admins. This allows them to do things like send out broadcast messages, control chat rooms, and other things:

```
{access, announce, [{allow, admin}]}.
{access, configure, [{allow, admin}]}.
{acl, admin, {user, "admin", "example.com"}}.
```

Note that it does not define the user itself, rather it just allows any user defined by that **Jabber ID (JID)** to be part of the admin group. The user itself in our case is defined by its existence as a local user account, so you'll want to make sure that your admin user is an actual system user as well.

We also restrict access to the configuration and announce services to just the admin group in order to prevent other users from reconfiguring the service or sending broadcast messages.

Modules

The last major piece is the modules load list, which defines what optional pieces of functionality we want to enable:

```
{modules,
 [
  {mod_adhoc,      []},
  {mod_announce,   [{access, announce}]},
  {mod_blocking,[]},
  {mod_caps,       []},
  {mod_configure,[]},
  {mod_disco,      []},
  {mod_http_bind,  []},
  {mod_last,       []},
  {mod_muc,        [
                    {host, "conference.@HOST@"},
                    {access, muc},
                    {access_create, muc_create},
                    {access_persistent, muc_create},
                    {access_admin, muc_admin}
                   ]},
  {mod_offline,   [{access_max_user_messages,
                     max_user_offline_messages}]},
  {mod_ping,       []},
  {mod_privacy,    []},
  {mod_private,    []},
  {mod_pubsub,     [
                    {access_createnode, pubsub_createnode},
                    {ignore_pep_from_offline, true},
                    {last_item_cache, false},
                    {plugins, ["flat", "hometree", "pep"]}
                   ]},
  {mod_roster,     []},
  {mod_shared_roster,[]},
  {mod_stats,      []},
  {mod_time,       []},
  {mod_vcard,      []},
  {mod_version,    []}
 ]}.
```

We are only going to look at a couple of the bigger modules here, but the rest are defined within the ejabberd installation and operations guide: `https://www.ejabberd.im/files/doc/guide.html`.

mod_muc

mod_muc implements the Multi-User Chat functionality defined by XEP-0045, although you may know them as chat rooms. We define a virtual hostname for the MUC service, which in this case would be `conference.example.com` (defined as `conference.@HOST@` in order to support servers hosting multiple domains.

We also define which access control group is able to create (`muc_create`), manage (`muc_admin`), or join chat rooms (`muc`). The access control settings limit to local users, admin users, and all users, respectively:

```
{access, muc_admin, [{allow, admin}]}.
{access, muc_create, [{allow, local}]}.
{access, muc, [{allow, all}]}.
```

mod_roster

mod_roster enables the creation of buddy groups within your chat client. This is necessary if you're building a chat system, but perhaps less important if you're just using ejabberd as a general XML message passing system.

mod_announce

mod_announce allows users on the correct access control group (admin in our example) to send broadcast messages to all logged-in users. This may be a useful feature for a small server full of trusted users, or it is a potential for abuse for larger servers if it is available to more than just admins.

Configuring DNS for XMPP

Much like an e-mail server, there are special DNS records which you can optionally add to your zone file in order to change how the XMPP service operates.

How to do it...

1. Add the c2s service to DNS:

   ```
   _xmpp-client._tcp 28800 IN SRV 20 0 5222 xmpp.example.com.
   ```

2. Add the s2s service to DNS:

   ```
   _xmpp-server._tcp 28800 IN SRV 20 0 5269 xmpp.example.com.
   ```

How it works...

Similar to an e-mail, XMPP can use normal A records (or CNAMEs) for a given domain to handle message delivery if the messages are going to be defined to the IP for the root of the domain. In other words, if `user@example.com` will be hosted on a server which example.com points to directly, then it will work fine.

Also similar to an e-mail, it often makes sense to have the traffic served by a different machine. Rather than MX records which are mail-specific, XMPP uses SRV records, which are a more general approach to looking up a service.

The SRV records are in the format of:

 ▸ **Service**: The predefined service name that someone will look up. Clients will automatically attempt to look up `_xmpp-client`, while servers for s2s communication will look up `_xmpp-server`.

 ▸ **Protocol**: This may be `_tcp` or `_udp`.

 ▸ **TTL**: The TTL for the DNS record. The longer the TTL the less DNS traffic you'll see, but the longer it will take to perform a failover.

 ▸ **IN SRV**: This is the record type (SRV).

 ▸ **Priority**: If you have multiple servers serving a domain, then you can choose to put them at the same priority or a different priority depending on if they're used for failover or live load splitting. This works like it would in an MX record. Lower priorities are preferred.

 ▸ **Weight**: An additional preference on top of the priority. Higher weights are preferred.

 ▸ **Port**: The port for your service. We're just going to define the normal defaults here, but you can choose to send your traffic over non-standard ports, and clients which obey the standards should connect properly.

 ▸ **Target**: The machine which will actually accept the connection. This can be a CNAME or an A/AAAA record.

Configuring the Pidgin client

While using XMPP as an XML message passing system is becoming more and more common, the original use was using it for user-to-user chatting. With this use case, you'll want to use client software for accessing the service.

One common open source XMPP client is Pidgin. Pidgin was initially created as the GTK+ AIM client, or GAIM. Over time, gaim gained the ability to implement additional protocols via a plugin architecture. In 2007, **gaim** was renamed **pidgin** in response to the legal pressures from America Online, who owned a trademark on the name AIM.

Pidgin plugins can also implement other pieces of functionality including an implementation of the **Off the Record** (**OTR**) protocol, which allows for end-to-end encryption of chat messages layered over the underlying protocol.

In addition to making protocols available as plugins, Pidgin split its core chat functionality into a separate library called **libpurple**, which was then adopted by other client implementations as well.

Pidgin is available on Windows, most Linux distributions, BSDs, and on Mac OS X. On OS X, you might prefer to look at Adium instead, which is a native OS X application using Pidgin's libpurple library for protocol support.

Lets take a look at how to use Pidgin to connect to our XMPP server.

How to do it...

The install process here is going to be a bit different since we're going to be installing Pidgin on what is essentially a client system rather than the server that we've been working on setting up. The client system itself may be Windows, Mac or another Linux system though, so we'll talk briefly about installing on each platform.

Install pidgin

If you are using Pidgin on an Ubuntu desktop, you can install it with `sudo apt-get install pidgin`. For Windows systems, you'll want to download and run the Windows installer from `http://www.pidgin.im`. For Mac OS X, it may be installed via source or through the MacPorts or Homebrew projects.

Configuring your account

Upon first launch, Pidgin will prompt you to add an account:

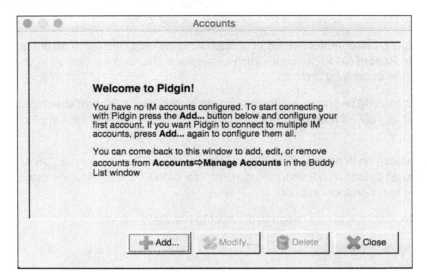

After selecting **Add**, you'll see a screen that allows you to select the protocol and various configuration options:

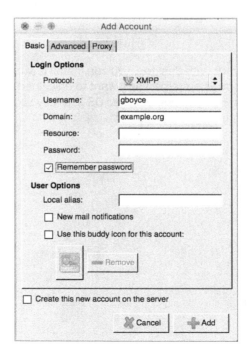

Setting the username and domain should be enough in our case. Pidgin will use the SRV records that we previously configured to locate and connect to your XMPP server instance.

If the XMPP SRV records were not in place, then Pidgin would attempt to connect to the A record for example.org, which may or may not be the right system. If example.org is not the correct system to connect to, then you can override the server to connect to by setting the Connect Server under the **Advanced** tab:

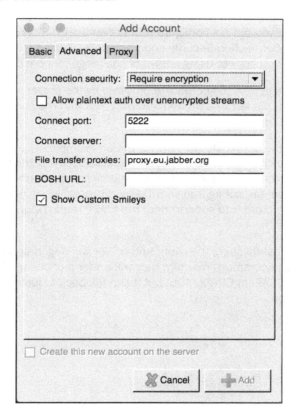

Once connected, you will be able to chat with any other user on the system, or use various built-in server functionalities, such as the **Multi-User Chat** (**MUC**) rooms. Additionally, if you previously configured XMPP S2S connections, you can exchange messages with users on other public XMPP servers.

How it works...

Once the account is configured, Pidgin will attempt to determine how to connect to the specified domain. It will start by attempting to look up the SRV record `for_xmpp-client._tcp.example.org`. If that DNS record does not exist, it will attempt to find the A record for example.org and direct connect to the returned address.

In the default configuration, Pidgin will attempt to connect via port 5222 while requiring TLS support via STARTTLS. If you did not configure your server with TLS certificates, you'll need to change the settings for Connection Security and potentially check *Allow plaintext auth over unencrypted streams* if you are not using a form of challenge response authentication.

Assuming TLS support is in use, the certificate provided by the server will be validated to confirm that it is properly signed by a trusted authority and that the common name of the certificate is valid for its usage.

The common name for the certificate will need to match example.org in our default configuration, which uses SRV records. If instead you are specifying the Connect Server in the advanced tab, then the server certificate must match the hostname specified in that field. Often, XMPP servers are configured with TLS certificates, which specify **Subject Alternate Names** (**SAN**) in order to support both the XMPP realm (`example.org`) and the server name itself.

Once the connection is established, the client and server will negotiate an authentication protocol that they have in common. Typically, they will prefer a challenge/response SASL mechanism, such as GSSAPI or CRAM-MD5, but it can fall back to just sending the password itself over the connection.

10
Monitoring Your Network

In this chapter, we will cover:

- ▸ Installing Nagios
- ▸ Adding Nagios users
- ▸ Adding Nagios hosts
- ▸ Monitoring services
- ▸ Defining commands
- ▸ Monitoring via NRPE
- ▸ Monitoring via SNMP

Introduction

While a bit less common for home networks, monitoring is one of the key responsibilities of a systems administrator in the business world. A good `sysadmin` should be aware of failures in the systems that they're responsible for before the end user notices the problems. In fact, they are often aware of issues before they occur, due to monitoring resources to detect bottlenecks before they trigger any service degradation.

Monitoring can fall into a number of categories, including graphing, alerting, and in some cases, automated fixes.

Installing Nagios

Nagios is an industry standard for open source monitoring and reporting. It is incredibly flexible and extendable, for better or worse. Getting it set up and running is not too difficult, but additional thought and understanding both Nagios and the systems which you would like to monitor will be necessary in order to create a configuration which is easy to understand and maintain.

How to do it...

1. Install `nagios`:

   ```
   sudo apt-get install nagios3
   ```

2. Select a password when prompted.

3. Visit the web UI at `http://YOURSERVER/nagios3/`. You can log in using `nagiosadmin` as a username, and the password, which you selected in the previous step. Since this system requires you to log in, you'll want to follow the instructions in the Apache chapter to configure and require SSL/TLS for the system.

How it works...

Debian and Ubuntu have done most of the hard work of determining how to configure Nagios for you. Once you install the `nagios3` meta package and all of its dependencies, you automatically get a configured Nagios system which is functional and already configured to monitor the local system.

Adding Nagios users

Nagios automatically creates the `nagiosadmin` user with full access rights to the system, but if you're operating in a larger environment, you will likely want to provide additional user accounts for other users to connect to. This will allow you to use a finer grained access control as well as making your life easier, as employees come and go in the company.

How to do it...

1. Create the user account:

   ```
   htpasswd /etc/nagios3/htpasswd.users user
   ```

2. Alternatively, you can reconfigure Apache to use system authentication for Nagios by editing `/etc/apache2/conf-available/nagios3` to read:

   ```
   <IfModule mod_authnz_external.c>
           AddExternalAuth pwauth /usr/sbin/pwauth
   ```

```
        SetExternalAuthMethod pwauth pipe
</IfModule>

<DirectoryMatch (/usr/share/nagios3/htdocs|/usr/lib/cgi-bin/
nagios3|/etc/nagios3/stylesheets)>
        Options FollowSymLinks
        DirectoryIndex index.php index.html
        AllowOverride AuthConfig
        Order Allow,Deny
        Allow From All
        AuthName "Nagios Access"
        AuthType Basic
        AuthBasicProvider external
        AuthExternal pwauth
        require valid-user
</DirectoryMatch>
```

3. Define a contact for the user by editing:

   /etc/nagios3/conf.d/contacts_nagios2.cfg.

4. Add the user to the admin contact group.

5. Restart nagios3:

   sudo service nagios3 restart

How it works...

There are two pieces to this configuration:

- ▶ **Authentication**: This just refers to the process of confirming that a user is who they say they are. Nagios leaves authentication to the Apache process. The stock install leverages Apache's htpasswd tool to manage a file, which defines a set of usernames and passwords. You can instead choose to tie Apache into another authentication source like Active Directory, LDAP, or just use system authentication like the one we did in the WebDAV example.

- ▶ **Authorization**: This defines what the given user has access to do. The default configuration allows any authenticated user to access the web UI, but content about actual hosts and configuration is restricted to users who are given access rights.

There are several ways to grant access to a given user:

- ▶ `/etc/nagios3/cgi.cfg`: This is the way that the `nagi`osadmin user gains its access rights. Among other configuration settings, this file contains variables that define who is authorized to access system information, configuration information, system commands, all services, all hosts, all service commands, or all host commands.

- ▶ Within a service definition, you can specify either a contact or a contact group defined within `/etc/nagios3/conf.d/contacts_nagios2.cfg` to give rights to.

- ▶ Within a host definition, you can also choose a contact or a contact group.

- ▶ Between these three options, you have good flexibility for defining both who has access rights to monitor assets and who should be notified for pre-defined alerts.

Adding Nagios hosts

Monitoring the local system is different than monitoring remote systems. A big part of this is that while monitoring your local system, you have full access to information regarding number of processes, amount of memory, CPU usage, and so on. When you're looking at remote systems, you're limited to accessing remotely accessible information like if a remote port is listening, ping ability, and so on. If you require the ability to collect more in depth information, you'll need to configure something to make the additional information available.

How to do it...

You can configure additional hosts to be monitored by Nagios by creating additional host entry in a `.cfg` file within `/etc/nagios3/conf.d/`.

The content should be:

```
define host {
        use                     generic-host
        host_name               testbox
        hostgroups              http-servers,ssh-servers
}
```

While multiple machines may be defined within the same `.cfg` file, separate files per machine may make more sense for future manageability. You can also choose to put the files within a subdirectory of `conf.d` that Nagios will automatically detect. I like to put my hosts into `/etc/nagios3/conf.d/hosts`.

How it works...

The host definition works using `generic-host` as a template for the host and then overriding values from that template as needed. The generic-host template is defined within `/etc/nagios3/conf.d/generic-host_nagios2.cfg`. These templates work by just existing as a defined host, but with `register` set as `0` so that Nagios does not attempt to monitor them directly.

Next, we define a `host_name` for the host. This setting is used in a variety of ways, including acting as a unique identifier for the host within Nagios configurations, as the name displayed within Nagios (unless overridden by a `display_name` setting), and as the hostname to attempt to collect data from (unless overridden by an address setting).

Finally, we have an optional **hostgroups** definition, which defines some groups which the machine is a member of for easier service configuration. If desired, you can also add the host to a hostgroup through the hostgroup definition itself. You'll want to consider what makes more sense for longer term manageability.

Monitoring services

A **service** in `nagios` defines a particular test which should be run. At a minimum you need to define a name for the service and the command to run in order to monitor it.

Similar to hosts, it is defined within `.cfg` files in `/etc/nagios3/conf.d` or a subdirectory. At a technical level, there is no difference between a `.cfg` file that defines a host versus one that defines a service. They are split in Ubuntu's default configuration just for ease of management. If you wanted to, you could have a single flat `.cfg` that defines all hosts, services, and users.

How to do it...

Again I like to split my services into a subdirectory, so let's look at defining a service to monitor HP Jetdirect printers by creating `/etc/nagios3/conf.d/services/printer.cfg` containing:

```
define hostgroup {
        hostgroup_name printers
}

define service {
        hostgroup_name                  printers
        service_description             jetdirect
        check_command                   check_hpjd
```

```
        use                       generic-service
        notification_interval     0
}
```

How it works...

Here we've defined a new hostgroup with a name of printers in order to be able to more easily add additional printers in the future. This hostgroup configuration could also exist in `hostgroups_nagios2.cfg`, but for our purposes it makes sense to co-exist with the service itself.

Next, we define the service itself, basing it upon the generic-service template defined in `generic-service_nagios2.cfg`. We then give it a service description, which must be unique for a given server. You may have multiple services with the same name as long as they do not apply to the same systems, but you may want to avoid this in order to avoid confusion.

Next, we define the `check_command`, which is the command that we're going to run in order to collect the data on a given service. Our example is the `check_hpjd` command, which uses the HP Jetdirect protocol to collect information about a remote printer. Hewlett-Packard created the protocol for their printers, but a number of other printer vendors implement the protocol as well.

Some commands accept arguments, which are defined by separating them by ! characters. For example, `check_users` checks a warning threshold for the first argument and a critical threshold for a second argument. These are passed in your `check_command` definition by writing `check_users!20!50`.

Defining commands

The commands that you may use for a given service need to be defined as well. The commands are defined within `/etc/nagios-plugins/config`, which is also included by `/etc/nagios3/nagios.cfg`.

This is a useful place to look if you want to see how an existing command is defined, or if you want to define your own custom command.

How to do it...

Let's create a custom command that uses an existing plugin to monitor a new service. Plex media servers are configured by default to use a web server configured on port 32400. So let's define a `check_plex` service that uses `check_http` on port 32400.

To do this, we're going to create /etc/nagios-plugins/config/plex.cfg:

```
define command{
        command_name    check_plex
        command_line    /usr/lib/nagios/plugins/check_http -H
'$HOSTADDRESS$' -I '$HOSTADDRESS$' -p 32400 '$ARG1$'
        }
```

How it works...

Command definitions are simple. You provide a command name and then the command you're going to execute on the local box in order to collect data.

There are a number of macros that are available to put into the configuration, including the $HOSTADDRESS$ and $ARG1$ settings we used previously. $HOSTADDRESS$ is populated by the host_name or address variables within the host definition. $ARG1$ is populated by the first argument specified in the call to check_plex (if defined). We can then pass any macros we want to the check_http command, which the nagios daemon will call.

Monitoring via NRPE

As I mentioned earlier, a number of plugins, such as check_memory, collect information from the system itself, which means that they cannot be directly used for monitoring remote systems. As these are often critical things to monitor, there are ways available to indirectly collect that information from remote systems using the **Nagios Remote Plugin Executer** (**NRPE**).

NRPE runs on the machine that you'd like to monitor and executes the same commands/plugins which Nagios itself would have. Nagios is then configured to collect data from NRPE rather than collecting data directly.

How to do it...

1. Install nrpe on your monitoring target:

   sudo apt-get install nagios-nrpe-server

2. Restrict access to the NRPE service:

   sed -i 's|allowed_hosts=.*|allowed_hosts=192.168.1.0/24|g' /etc/nagios/nrpe.cfg

3. Define any additional checks to run by adding them into /etc/nagios/nrpe.cfg:

   command[check_raid]=/usr/lib/nagios/plugins/check_raid

4. Configure your `nagios` server to collect data via `nrpe` by creating `/etc/nagios3/conf.d/linux-servers.cfg`:

```
define hostgroup {
        hostgroup_name linux-servers
}

define service {
        hostgroup_name          linux-servers
        service_description     Check Users
        check_command           check_nrpe_1arg!check_users
        use                     generic-service
        notification_interval   0
}
```

How it works...

There are two major parts to using NRPE: configuring the NRPE services in your remote machine and configuring Nagios to use NRPE for collecting data.

On the target

There are two major parts to using NRPE: configuring the NRPE services in your remote machine and configuring Nagios to use NRPE for collecting data.

When configuring NRPE itself on the remote hosts, you'll want to ensure that your `allowed_hosts` definition is as restrictive as possible, while still allowing all your monitoring systems to talk to it in order to avoid allowing random people to collect data about your systems. Additional protections, such as firewall rules, may not be a bad idea as well.

When it comes to the commands which `nrpe` will execute, configuration is a lot simpler than it is with Nagios, but less flexible. Your service definition specifies the name of the command (`check_raid`) and the command which will be executed, including any arguments.

Since any macros defined on your Nagios server would need to be passed to NRPE over the network, support for command line arguments to commands is discouraged. This is to avoid allowing attackers to execute arbitrary commands remotely. Instead, the commands will be configured in a manner that is either specified to the host, or generic enough to have the desired behavior on any system.

On the Nagios host

Monitoring on the Nagios server side is handled just like it would be for any other service. The only difference is that the command being executed is `check_nrpe_1arg`, and its first argument is the command to execute on the remote host.

If you need to pass arguments to the remote NRPE daemon, they can be passed by using `check_nrpe` instead and passing it as an additional argument. For example, `check_nrpe!check_custom!-a arguments`.

Monitoring via SNMP

In addition to using NRPE to collect data, Nagios can also collect data via SNMP (Simple Network Management Protocol). This is especially useful for monitoring network equipment like routers and switches, which often have SNMP agents built into them.

How to do it...

1. Install the Nagios SNMP plugins:

    ```
    sudo apt-get install nagios-snmp-plugins
    ```

2. Define some SNMP checks using SNMPv2:

    ```
    define hostgroup {
            hostgroup_name snmp-hosts
    }

    define service {
            hostgroup_name              snmp-hosts
            service_description         Load Average
            check_command               \ check_snmp_load_
    v2!netsc!30!40!!public
            use                         generic-service
            notification_interval       0
    }

    define service {
            hostgroup_name              snmp-hosts
            service_description         Interface Status
            check_command               \ check_snmp_int_
    v2!!!public
            use                         generic-service
            notification_interval       0
    }

    define service {
            hostgroup_name              snmp-hosts
            service_description         Memory Usage
            check_command               \ check_snmp_mem_
    v2!!90,20!95,30!!public
            use                         generic-service
            notification_interval       0
    }
    ```

How it works...

Our example here assumes that you're monitoring a network device that already has SNMP enabled. Additionally, it must use the community string of public. If you wish to use a different community string, then you'll need to replace public with the correct value in the preceding example.

Each of the `check_snmp_*` commands that we use here are defined in `/usr/share/nagios-snmp-plugins/pluginconfig/snmp_*.cfg` and use scripts installed by the `nagios-snmp-plugins` package. You can look at the `.cfg` file in order to determine the correct order of arguments.

Unused arguments can be left blank. For example, Memory Usage uses `check_snmp_mem_v2`, which is defined by `/usr/share/nagios-snmp-plugins/pluginconfig/snmp_mem.cfg` as:

```
define command {
        command_name check_snmp_mem_v2
        command_line $USER1$/check_snmp_mem.pl -H $HOSTADDRESS$ -C
$ARG5$ -2 $ARG1$ -w $ARG2$ -c $ARG3$ $ARG4$
}
```

Reading the preceding setting, you can see that the first argument is used right after `-2` (use snmpv2), which itself doesn't take any arguments. `$ARG1$` instead can be used for passing arbitrary options. `$ARG2$` defines the warning threshold (`-w`). `$ARG3$` defines the community string (`-c`). Finally, `$ARG4$` may also be used for specifying arbitrary options at the end of the command line.

11
Mapping Your Network

In this chapter, we are going to cover:

- ► Detecting systems on your network with NMAP
- ► Detecting Systems Using Arp-Scan
- ► Scanning TCP ports
- ► Scanning UDP ports
- ► Identifying services
- ► Identifying operating systems

Introduction

Modern home and small business networks are not the simple things they once were with only a handful of devices on them. Between the **Internet of Things** (**IoT**), streaming video devices, microcomputers such as the Raspberry Pi, and phones/tablets, you can expect your network to contain dozens of utilized IP addresses.

If you want to have a good security posture on your network, having a good understanding of what exists is critical. If you do not understand what exists, then you cannot understand what should not be there. This could mean an unpatched system that you forgot about, or it could mean an intruder on your network.

In this chapter, we will be talking about some of the various steps you can take in order to better inventory your network and what tools you should use in order to do it.

Detecting systems on your network with NMAP

If you have heard of `nmap` before, it was likely as a **hacker** tool. These days it is most commonly used as a port scanner, but it actually started its life as a network-mapping tool for discovering hosts. In fact, **nmap** stands for **Network Mapper**. It can utilize ICMP, UDP, and TCP.

Let us look at how to utilize it to discover what systems exist on your network.

How to do it...

First, we need to make sure that we have `nmap` installed. Luckily, it is a common enough tool to be available in the package repository for your selected distribution, and it will be accessible either by running sudo apt-get install `nmap` or sudo yum install `nmap`.

Next, we will do a simple ICMP sweep of the network to see who responds:

```
# nmap -sP 10.0.0.0/24
Starting Nmap 6.40 ( http://nmap.org ) at 2016-05-03 15:43 EDT
Nmap scan report for 10.0.0.1
Host is up (0.00053s latency).
MAC Address: 52:54:00:65:7D:0A (QEMU Virtual NIC)
Nmap scan report for 10.0.0.10
Host is up.
Nmap done: 256 IP addresses (2 hosts up) scanned in 2.06 seconds
```

Overall, it is a bit boring, since all our network contains is our router and the single client system. Things get a bit interesting when we scan a larger network:

```
# nmap   -n -sP 192.168.1.0/24

Starting Nmap 6.40 ( http://nmap.org ) at 2016-05-03 15:49 EDT
Nmap scan report for 192.168.1.1
Host is up (0.00041s latency).
MAC Address: E8:DE:27:BA:D0:BE (Tp-link Technologies Co.)
Nmap scan report for 192.168.1.105
Host is up (-0.100s latency).
MAC Address: 00:17:88:14:44:7D (Philips Lighting BV)
Nmap scan report for 192.168.1.115
Host is up (0.25s latency).
```

```
MAC Address: 00:04:20:F1:4D:1D (Slim Devices)
Nmap scan report for 192.168.1.117
Host is up (0.010s latency).
MAC Address: C8:E0:EB:16:EE:93 (Apple)
...
Nmap scan report for 192.168.1.254
Host is up (0.00034s latency).
MAC Address: 60:E3:27:49:1C:5E (Unknown)
Nmap scan report for 192.168.1.237
Host is up.
Nmap done: 256 IP addresses (32 hosts up) scanned in 4.23 seconds
```

How it works...

Nmap allows you to scan IP addresses by specifying an IP Address, a CIDR block, or a range (for example, 192.168.1.10-20). You can even specify multiples of each on the command line in order to increase the number of targets of your scan.

The -s argument allows you to specify the scan type. We are using -sP, which tells nmap to do a ping scan. Also supported are SYN scans, TCP Connect scans, UDP scans, and so on.

During a ping scan of a remote network, nmap sends ICMP echo requests to all of the target hosts, listening for ICMP echo responses from the target. For each host that responds from within the specified ranges, the latency is provided.

If you are scanning a local network then the ICMP echo requests are replaced by ARP requests. This has the benefit of being able to find systems that are configured to ignore ICMP packets. If you are running a local scan as the root user, then you will get the MAC address of the responding systems in the scan results as well, as shown by our preceding output.

The vendor identification works as a function of the MAC address. The first half of a given MAC address is a unique vendor identifier assigned by The Institute of Electrical and Electronics Engineers, or IEEE. The mapping of MAC address prefix to vendor is made available online for free by the organization, and various tools may be found online for looking up the manufacturer of a given MAC.

Detecting Systems Using Arp-Scan

Some systems choose to block the ICMP traffic, which can result in them not appearing in a ping scan. Any system on your local network, however, must respond to ARP requests if they are going to communicate with additional machines on the network. This gives you an additional option for system enumeration when you are on the local network segment.

How to do it...

First, you install a tool, which will allow you to issue arbitrary `arp` requests. There are many tools like this, but we are going to use `arp-scan`, since it allows you to specify entire netblocks rather than just individual IP addresses:

```
$ sudo apt-get install arp-scan
```

Now you can actually use the tool to scan your local network segment:

```
$ sudo arp-scan  192.168.1.0/24
Interface: eth0, datalink type: EN10MB (Ethernet)
Starting arp-scan 1.8.1 with 256 hosts (http://www.nta-monitor.com/tools/
arp-scan/)
192.168.1.1      44:d9:e7:9b:a2:9d     (Unknown)
192.168.1.2      40:8d:5c:4b:85:d9     (Unknown)
192.168.1.105     00:17:88:14:44:7d      Philips Lighting BV
192.168.1.129     00:1f:bc:11:99:13      EVGA Corporation
192.168.1.164     40:8d:5c:59:d6:50     (Unknown)
192.168.1.156     74:75:48:29:b1:fa     (Unknown)
192.168.1.178     00:d9:d1:26:3a:ea     (Unknown)
192.168.1.191     d0:52:a8:53:f3:07     (Unknown)
192.168.1.193     d8:cb:8a:1b:8a:b1     (Unknown)
192.168.1.116     00:04:20:f3:d0:7a      Slim Devices, Inc.
192.168.1.125     74:75:48:15:b9:95     (Unknown)
192.168.1.216     fc:aa:14:d9:ef:c0     (Unknown)
192.168.1.224     80:2a:a8:13:15:93     (Unknown)
192.168.1.207     c8:e0:eb:16:ee:93     (Unknown)
192.168.1.205     74:da:ea:f3:ff:07     (Unknown)
192.168.1.227     8c:e2:da:f0:52:22     (Unknown)
192.168.1.229     a4:1f:72:ff:0e:77     (Unknown)
192.168.1.233     52:54:00:34:21:f6      QEMU
192.168.1.236     08:00:27:f5:28:d1      CADMUS COMPUTER SYSTEMS
192.168.1.239     70:56:81:a3:d4:43     (Unknown)
192.168.1.188     80:1f:02:7e:73:0e      Edimax Technology Co. Ltd.
192.168.1.243     0c:4d:e9:ce:fc:0b     (Unknown)
192.168.1.117     00:04:20:f1:4d:1d      Slim Devices, Inc.
```

192.168.1.141	00:01:36:43:4f:a9	CyberTAN Technology, Inc.
192.168.1.192	d0:e7:82:7c:88:ef	(Unknown)
192.168.1.159	b8:3e:59:15:78:65	(Unknown)
192.168.1.254	60:e3:27:49:1c:5e	(Unknown)
192.168.1.131	84:a4:66:34:d2:63	(Unknown)
192.168.1.206	64:bc:0c:46:bf:c1	(Unknown)
192.168.1.208	00:80:92:b0:d4:f2	Silex Technology, Inc.
192.168.1.154	78:4b:87:70:37:56	(Unknown)
192.168.1.210	74:75:48:8b:01:3e	(Unknown)
192.168.1.211	64:bc:0c:2e:4f:55	(Unknown)
192.168.1.165	00:11:d9:a2:c6:7e	TiVo

```
36 packets received by filter, 0 packets dropped by kernel
Ending arp-scan 1.8.1: 256 hosts scanned in 1.216 seconds (210.53 hosts/
sec). 34 responded
```

How it works...

ARP scans are very simple. The utility simply has to send a broadcast ARP request packet which asks who has a particular IP address. Any listening system configured for that IP address will send a broadcast ARP response that provides the MAC address that owns that IP address. If multiple systems believe that they own the IP (for example in an IP conflict), then they will both respond to the request.

An upside to this scan approach is that it is simple/quick to use, allowing you to scan large local networks in a fast manner. It is also more effective than a ping scan, since it will detect systems that are blocking ICMP traffic.

The downside is that this approach only works on the local layer 2 network. Since ARP packets are never routed, the scan cannot be used to scan a network which you are *not* physically connected to.

Scanning TCP ports

Now that we have identified which systems exist, we can look at what services exist on those hosts. We will start with TCP services, since they are much easier to understand the results for.

There are a number of different types of TCP scans, but we are going to look at the two most common ones, the Connect scan and the SYN scan.

How to do it...

The two most common types of scans used for detecting open TCP ports are TCP Connect Scans, and SYN scans. SYN scans are the stealthier and potentially safer option, but require root privileges to run. Let's look at both and see how they differ.

TCP CONNECT scan

Let's start the TCP CONNECT scan:

```
$ nmap -sT 10.0.0.10

Starting Nmap 6.40 ( http://nmap.org ) at 2016-05-06 15:14 EDT
Nmap scan report for 10.0.0.10
Host is up (0.0016s latency).
Not shown: 994 closed ports
PORT     STATE SERVICE
22/tcp   open  ssh
25/tcp   open  smtp
80/tcp   open  http
111/tcp  open  rpcbind
139/tcp  open  netbios-ssn
445/tcp  open  microsoft-ds

Nmap done: 1 IP address (1 host up) scanned in 0.14 seconds
```

TCP SYN scan

Let's start the TCP SYN scan:

```
$ sudo nmap -sS 10.0.0.10

Starting Nmap 6.40 ( http://nmap.org ) at 2016-05-06 15:15 EDT
Nmap scan report for 10.0.0.10
Host is up (0.000069s latency).
Not shown: 994 closed ports
PORT     STATE SERVICE
22/tcp   open  ssh
25/tcp   open  smtp
80/tcp   open  http
111/tcp  open  rpcbind
139/tcp  open  netbios-ssn
445/tcp  open  microsoft-ds
MAC Address: 52:54:00:A7:A4:19 (QEMU Virtual NIC)

Nmap done: 1 IP address (1 host up) scanned in 1.66 seconds
```

How it works...

The TCP CONNECT scans are the default type of scan if you are running as a non-root user. Much like any other application attempting to connect to a TCP port, it issues a connect request that tells the operating system to do a normal 3-way TCP handshake, closing the connection if it is accepted.

SYN scans are a stealthier scan, opting to complete only steps 1 and 2 of the TCP handshake before sending a reset packet in order to abort the attempt. This means that the application, which is bound to the port, does not ever see an established connection, so it will not log the connection attempt. It is also potentially safer, since historically, some applications have not dealt well with connections being opened and then closed by a port scan.

Since SYN scans do not perform the full TCP handshake, like the Linux kernel would do by default, they require access to RAW sockets, which is typically restricted to root. RAW sockets allow an application to craft and send their own custom packets, which allows you the ability to skirt various rules of network traffic. Once you are a root user for the scan, nmap will select SYN scans by default.

Additional TCP scans are available, for example, the FIN scan, Null scan, or the X-Mas scan. These scan types tend to be less generally useful; however, you may find interest in reading more about them later.

Scanning UDP ports

It is very easy to read the results of a TCP scan due to its stateful nature. A SYN packet will always be answered with a FIN if the port is closed or a SYN/ACK if the port is opened. The lack of a response means that either the request or its response was filtered.

UDP is not so easy, due to it being stateless. A UDP packet to a closed port will result in an ICMP Destination Port Unreachable message. A filtered UDP packet will result in no response. The tricky part is that the behavior when something is listening to the port is application specific. Since there is no initial handshake, the application simply receives the data and then either responds or not depending on the application's requirements. If the application does not respond, it will look just like a filtered port.

How to do it...

Similar to SYN scans, UDP scans require root privileges. Simply use -sU in order to specify UDP for the scan type.

Before we run the scan, let's add UDP filtering on port 22 in order to see how it looks in the results:

```
$ sudo iptables -A INPUT -p udp -m udp --sport 22 -j DROP
```

Now, let's perform the scan:

```
$ sudo nmap -sU -p 1-100 10.0.0.10


Starting Nmap 6.40 ( http://nmap.org ) at 2016-05-08 14:40 EDT
Nmap scan report for 10.0.0.10
Host is up (0.00067s latency).
Not shown: 97 closed ports
PORT    STATE          SERVICE
22/udp open|filtered ssh
53/udp open            domain
68/udp open|filtered dhcpc
MAC Address: 52:54:00:A7:A4:19 (QEMU Virtual NIC)


Nmap done: 1 IP address (1 host up) scanned in 107.49 seconds
```

How it works...

The preceding UDP scan shows all four potential scenarios in its result.

The majority of the UDP ports on this system do not have applications listening on them. You can see this in the line which says *Not Shown: 97 Closed Ports*. Results from an nmap scan will automatically consolidate the answer, which occurs most often in order to cut down on the size of the output.

UDP port 22 in the preceding results shows a state of open|filtered. This means that the UDP packet did not result in an ICMP Port Unreachable error, which means that the packet was either accepted or dropped by a firewall. In our case, it was filtered in our iptables rule.

UDP port 53 in the preceding results shows as Open. This is due to bind9 currently being installed/running on that IP address. The UDP packet sent by nmap results in the bind9 server responding with NOTIMP, or Not Implemented. This means that the request type in the packet was not recognized, which makes sense, since it was not actually a DNS packet.

Finally, port 68 also shows `open|filtered`, just like port 22. In this case, it is due to port 68 being used by our DHCP client. The client does not bother responding to the packet, since it is a valid DHCP packet. You can determine what is listening with on a given UDP port using the `lsof` command:

```
# lsof -i udp:68
COMMAND    PID USER    FD    TYPE DEVICE SIZE/OFF NODE NAME
dhclient 1215 root     6u    IPv4   9362      0t0  UDP *:bootpc
```

Identifying services

Another useful piece of functionality that nmap provides is the ability to identify services by attempting to grab application banners or issue various types of known requests and determine the service based upon how it responds.

How to do it...

Use `-sV` to probe for service/version information:

```
$ nmap 10.0.0.10 -sV

Starting Nmap 6.40 ( http://nmap.org ) at 2016-05-08 16:15 EDT
Nmap scan report for 10.0.0.10
Host is up (0.0016s latency).
Not shown: 995 closed ports
PORT     STATE SERVICE VERSION
22/tcp   open  ssh      (protocol 2.0)
25/tcp   open  smtp    Postfix smtpd
53/tcp   open  domain
80/tcp   open  http    Apache httpd 2.4.7 ((Ubuntu))
111/tcp  open  rpcbind 2-4 (RPC #100000)
1 service unrecognized despite returning data. If you know the service/
version, please submit the following fingerprint at http://www.insecure.
org/cgi-bin/servicefp-submit.cgi :
SF-Port22-TCP:V=6.40%I=7%D=5/8%Time=572F9E4A%P=x86_64-pc-linux-
gnu%r(NULL,
SF:2B,"SSH-2\.0-OpenSSH_6\.6\.1p1\x20Ubuntu-2ubuntu2\.6\r\n");
Service Info: Host:  client

Service detection performed. Please report any incorrect results at
http://nmap.org/submit/ .
Nmap done: 1 IP address (1 host up) scanned in 11.23 seconds
```

How it works...

A version scan starts like a normal TCP connect scan, except established connections are used to look for banner strings (such as the SSH banner or the Postfix one). From there, nmap will look for banner strings and will send various types of requests (http, ftp, SSL handshakes, and so on) and try to identify services by the way that it responds. Either the result of this scan will identify the service, similar to Apache, or it will provide some details about the scan results, which may be submitted to Nmap's site for future identification.

Identifying operating systems

In addition to identifying services running on servers, nmap can additionally attempt to identify the Operating System running on a particular system. This type of scan typically requires at least one open and one closed port to be reached.

How to do it...

Use nmap -O to do OS fingerprinting:

```
$ sudo nmap -n -O 192.168.1.205 -p 22,80
Starting Nmap 6.40 ( http://nmap.org ) at 2016-05-20 17:57 EDT
Nmap scan report for 192.168.1.205
Host is up (0.013s latency).
PORT     STATE   SERVICE
22/tcp closed ssh
80/tcp open    http
MAC Address: 74:DA:EA:F3:FF:07 (Unknown)
Device type: general purpose
Running: Linux 2.6.X|3.X
OS CPE: cpe:/o:linux:linux_kernel:2.6 cpe:/o:linux:linux_kernel:3
OS details: Linux 2.6.32 - 3.2
Network Distance: 1 hop

OS detection performed. Please report any incorrect results at http://
nmap.org/submit/ .
Nmap done: 1 IP address (1 host up) scanned in 2.63 seconds
```

How it works...

Nmap's OS detection code works by issuing various packet types to services and looking at how the system responds. The proper response for a SYN packet is either a FIN or a SYN/ACK, but what is the proper response for a packet that makes no sense, like a TCP packet with no flags set? Since the behavior is not defined by the RFCs, it tends to vary based upon choices made by the developer. By observing the responses of a number of these unusual packet choices, nmap is able to narrow down which operating system is responding to the packets.

Some of the issued probes run to be done against open ports, while others run against closed ports. Due to this, you will find that the OS scan works best if the system has at least one open and one closed port available. A system that filters any closed ports will likely get much less reliable scan results.

Another problem to watch out for is scanning a system that is doing TCP port filtering to another system. If you are scanning a Linux router, which has port 80 forwarded to a Windows box, nmap will find the scan results rather confusing.

12

Watching Your Network

In this chapter, we are going to cover:

- ▶ Setting up centralized logging
- ▶ Installing a Snort IDS
- ▶ Managing your Snort rules
- ▶ Managing Snort logging

Introduction

Any network connected to the Internet can expect to see malicious traffic. Now, this could range anywhere from something like compromise of your system or an intruder connected to your network, or it could be something as simple as browsing the wrong website that attempts to use the latest Flash or Java exploit.

If your network is hosting anything of value, it may make sense for you to monitor this sort of traffic. It will allow you to notice the laptop infected with Malware that is probing your other systems.

Alternatively, maybe you just want to watch your network traffic in order to detect misconfigurations. Perhaps one of your systems is misconfigured, resulting in it hammering away at your server. IDS systems can be flexible enough to catch any sort of traffic that you would like to look for.

Setting up centralized logging

Linux servers are typically configured to use a syslog based logging system for handling events. There is a wide collection of syslog implementations, each with their own little take on log handling. By default, Ubuntu servers are configured with `rsyslog`, which is a fast and feature-full syslog implementation.

The configuration for `rsyslog` is defined in `/etc/rsyslog.conf`, as well as in any `*.conf` files included in `/etc/rsyslog.d/`. If you look in `/etc/rsyslog.d/50-default.conf`, you will see configuration entries, such as:

```
auth,authpriv.*                 /var/log/auth.log
*.*;auth,authpriv.none          -/var/log/syslog
```

The left-hand side shows the facility/severity of the syslog events. You can specify more than one of them using a comma separating the values. For example, `auth,authpriv.*` specified preceding logs both the `auth` and `authpriv` facilities at all severities to `/var/log/auth`. The syslog protocol allows for 24 different facilities (0-23), including ones dedicated for kernel messages, mail messages, user messages, and a variety of locally defined message types. The severity ranges from Emergency at severity 0, to Debug at severity 7.

The right-hand side shows the destination of the message. In both of these examples, the messages are being logged to a file. The first example logs messages to `/var/log/auth.log`. After each line is completed, the service calls *sync* in order to ensure that the messages are written to disk. The second example includes a – before `/var/log/syslog` in order to signify that the *sync* calls should be omitted. Logging with the *sync* calls omitted operates faster, but at the expense of potentially losing log entries during a system crash.

Input methods

The stock Ubuntu configuration only uses Unix Sockets and Kernel messages for receiving syslog data. Rsyslog itself is additionally have to read messages via TCP or UDP ports, through reading plaintext log files, or directly from system.

Output methods

Rsyslogd has more output options than it has input options. In addition to logging to plaintext files, `rsyslog` can log to a variety of databases, the systemd logger, pipes, SNMP, or to other syslog servers over TCP or UDP.

By setting a specific server to accept syslog messages via TCP or UDP, you can choose to forward copies of messages from all of your servers to a central logging location.

How to do it...

Configure your central server to accept messages via UDP by uncommenting the following lines in /etc/rsyslog.conf:

$ModLoad imudp

$UDPServerRun 514

Configure your other systems to forward their messages on to that system via UDP by adding the following to a file in /etc/rsyslogd.d/:

```
*.*      @10.0.0.1
```

How it works...

$ModLoad tells rsyslog to load a particular module. In this case, we're loading the UDP input module (imudp). In order for rsyslog to actually start listening though, you must define the port to listen on by setting $UDPServerRun. The UDP port assigned from the the the **Internet Assigned Numbers Authority** (**IANA**) is 514, so we are going to use that for the value.

On the logger side of the equation, things are much simpler. Just define the FACILITY. SEVERITY that you want to log remotely, and specify @TARGET. The target name can be a hostname or an IP address. In this case, I am forwarding messages to our router. It could very well make sense to have the log server be a dedicated box that even the router can send its messages to.

If you want to use TCP rather than UDP, you simply need to $ModLoad imtcp instead and define $InputTCPServerRun, and then specify your logging target as @@10.0.0.1 instead of @10.0.0.1. The choice between TCP and UDP will depend on your needs.

UDP is fast and does not require an established TCP connection, which could potentially be a limited resource on your system. More devices also very well support it since it, tends to be the default choice. As a downside however, it is trivial to spoof the source of, which could potentially lead to someone giving you false logs. It is also impossible to notice if you have dropped messages.

Using TCP instead provides you the additional reliability of a connection based protocol and the added spoof protection of the TCP three-way handshake. It can also be tunneled through proxies or wrapped in TLS to provide authentication of the server and client.

Installing a Snort IDS

To start monitoring our network for irregular traffic, we are going to start by installing a Snort IDS. Snort is one of the oldest and most feature packed Open Source **Network Intrusion Detection Systems** (**NIDS**). It is free for use, and there is a wide collection of rules freely available for it, as well as information and support on designing your own custom checks.

How to do it...

1. Install the snort daemon package:

    ```
    sudo apt-get install snort
    ```

2. When prompted, enter the network interface which you want to monitor. For our example, we will use eth0, which on our router is the LAN port.

3. Next, enter the network range which you consider local. We will use 10.0.0.0/24, which we previously defined as the LAN range. If desired, you can specify multiple CIDR blocks by having them comma separated without any whitespace.

How it works...

The network range(s) that you defined as local in the third step are used to populate the $HOME_NET setting within Snort. $HOME_NET and $EXTERNAL_NET are used within snort rules to allow you to specify the direction of the flow of packets which you care about.

Snort also wants to know what network interface it should put in promiscuous mode and listen on. Which interface you want to use has some rather interesting implications as to what you can see and how it will look.

WAN Interface

Your first instinct may be to monitor on your WAN interface, since it is externally facing. This is also very useful as it will allow you to detect attacks against any public facing services that you placed on the router box itself rather than forwarding to an internal server.

This approach will work, but it has some limitations. The main limitation is that even though monitoring from the WAN interface will show you any malicious traffic between a remote server and a computer behind your router, the traffic will always show the connection as being between the remote server and your router. This is because Snort is monitoring the external interface; it is seeing the packets before they are rewritten by the kernel. Therefore, you may discover that you have a compromised system on your network, but you will be unsure of which system it is without further investigation.

Another limitation of monitoring via the WAN interface is that your log will be very noisy. Any system connected to the Internet is under a constant barrage of malicious traffic from bots. There are systems out there infected with known viruses, worms, and rootkits, that may attempt to spread themselves automatically via automated SSH scans or attempts to exploit old vulnerabilities in software that you may or may not be running. Your IDS system will detect and log each of these attempts when they occur, and you may miss issues that you care about in the noise.

LAN interface

Monitoring the LAN interface allows you to see the internal IP address associated with a malicious request, but will miss any packets destined to the router itself from the Internet. It will, however, allow you to detect certain additional types of host-to-host communication on the internal network, such as ARP, DHCP, and other forms of broadcast traffic.

Dedicated interface

One limitation to using either the WAN or the LAN ports is that you will only detect traffic that passes through the router in some manner. If a machine on your network is compromised and is attacking the Internet, either approach will detect the traffic. However, if a compromised system on your network is attacking the other client systems on the network, that traffic will go unnoticed as long as they do not attack the router IP.

So, how do we see client-to-client traffic? Long ago, this was trivial on smaller networks, as the systems were often connected via hubs, which essentially turned all network traffic into broadcast traffic. Since the change to switched networks, the traffic became more isolated. Generally, this is a very good thing, but it does make our case here more complicated.

The best solution to this problem is Port Mirroring, which is a feature that is available in some better-managed switches. Port Mirroring, also called **Switched Port Analyzer** (**SPAN**) on Cisco gear, allows you to send a copy of all traffic on a given network port or VLAN to a specific network port. This allows you to plug a dedicated network interface on your system running Snort into it and then receive all the network traffic you want to see.

Note that port mirroring can potentially cause problems on high-traffic networks. If you are mirroring a VLAN containing 8 100Mb/s ports via a single 100Mb/s port, you can easily overwhelm the interface under load. Additionally, all of the traffic needs to pass through the switch's backplane and get processed by the switches CPU.

Another good point for using a dedicated network interface on your Snort box for monitoring is that it allows you to configure the network interface to be brought up without being configured with an IP address. By not providing an IP address on the monitoring port, you prevent people from addressing the device directly. In the case of a dedicated snort box, which is monitoring outside of your firewall, this could prevent someone from exploiting Snort and using the system to gain access to your internal network.

Managing your Snort rules

Your ability to monitor new threats is only as as good as your rules. When the latest Flash zero day starts being exploited actively, you will want to ensure that you get a new rule in place to detect it.

Luckily, Snort has a large user community and a support organization that writes rules and makes them available online. Their rules are broken into three sets: Community, Registered, and Subscription.

As the name implies, the Community set is created by the community and is hosted by `http://Snort.org` free. The registered and subscription sets are managed, tested, and improved by the company behind Snort. The paid Subscription set gives you access to rule updates 30 days earlier than the registered set, but otherwise the contents are identical.

Having a place to download rules from is great, but having a way to keep them up to date in an automated manner is even better. With Snort, this can be done by the PulledPork tool, which automates the downloads, installation, and management of the rule sets. Once you have registered for your account, you get access to a free Oinkcode, which is essentially an authorization key for downloading the rule sets. It is accessible when viewing your profile on `http://www.snort.org`.

How to do it...

1. Install `git`:

   ```
   $ sudo apt-get install git
   ```

2. Add libraries which `pulledpork` depends on:

   ```
   $ sudo apt-get install libcrypt-ssleay-perl
   ```

3. Clone the `git` repo:

   ```
   $ git clone https://github.com/shirkdog/pulledpork.git
   ```

4. Create a `pulledpork.conf` file:

   ```
   rule_url=https://snort.org/downloads/community/|community-rules.
   tar.gz|Community
   ignore=deleted.rules,experimental.rules,local.rules
   temp_path=/tmp
   rule_path=/etc/snort/rules/snort.rules
   local_rules=/etc/snort/rules/local.rules
   sid_msg=/etc/snort/sid-msg.map
   sid_msg_version=1
   sid_changelog=/var/log/sid_changes.log
   ```

```
snort_path=/usr/sbin/snort
config_path=/etc/snort/snort.conf
pid_path=/var/run/snort_eth0.pid
version=0.7.2
```

5. Run `pulledpork`:

```
$ sudo ./pulledpork.pl -T -H -c pulledpork.conf
Rules tarball download of community-rules.tar.gz....
Prepping rules from community-rules.tar.gz for work....
  Done!
Reading rules...
Setting Flowbit State....
  Done
Writing /etc/snort/rules/snort.rules....
  Done
Generating sid-msg.map....
  Done
Writing v1 /etc/snort/sid-msg.map....
  Done
HangUP Time....
  Done!
Writing /var/log/sid_changes.log....
  Done
Rule Stats...
  New:-------3415
  Deleted:---0
  Enabled Rules:----815
  Dropped Rules:----0
  Disabled Rules:---2600
  Total Rules:------3415
No IP Blacklist Changes

Done
Please review /var/log/sid_changes.log for additional details
Fly Piggy Fly!
```

How it works...

The `pulledpork` configuration, which we have defined here, tells it to download the community set of rules from snort.org and put them in place in `/etc/snort/rules`. We additionally pass in `-T`, which tells it to process text based rules, not .so based rules. We also pass `-H`, which tells `pulledpork` to automatically send a HUP signal to the snort process based upon the snort `pid` file which we provided via the `pid_path` variable.

Once the tarball is downloaded from the `rule_url` location, it is extracted, and the rules are placed in `/etc/snort/rules/snort.rules`. You may additionally specify config files with `-b` to disable specific rules, `-e` to enable non-default rules, or `-M` to modify the content of rules. These modifications may be triggered off the **Snort ID (SID)** of the rule, or through regular expression matching. You can look at examples of the configurations within `pulledpork/etc/`.

Within the `pulledpork.conf` file, you can also pull from the Registered/Subscription sets by specifying additional `rule_url` definitions that include your Oinkcode. For example:

```
rule_url=https://www.snort.org/reg-rules/|snortrules-snapshot.tar.
gz|<oinkcode>
```

Unfortunately, this is less useful on our Ubuntu 14.04 install due to the shipped version of Snort being no longer supported for new rules at snort.org. If you want to have the latest and greatest rules, consider building your own copy of Snort or installing a newer version of Ubuntu.

Managing Snort logging

The default Snort configuration causes it to log any triggered alerts in unified2 format to `/var/log/snort/snort.log`. This causes the alert instances and the relevant packet data to be logged in a binary format, which requires special tools to understand. One simple tool for reading unified2 format is `u2spewfoo`. Alternatively, `u2boat` can be used to convert the logs into `pcap` files, which may be read, by `tcpdump` or `wireshark`.

A useful option from the console without any non-Ubuntu provided tools would be to log alerts in plaintext to disk. These alert logs would allow you to easily read the messages from within `/var/log/snort` as plain text. You may also choose to have snort log packet captures directly in `pcap` format.

How to do it...

1. Open /etc/snort/snort.conf in your favorite text editor.

2. Search for the lines which start with *output* in order to determine the current logging settings and know where to put additional output options. The stock Ubuntu snort installation sets:

```
output unified2: filename snort.log, limit 128, nostamp, mpls_
event_types, vlan_event_types
```

3. Enable plaintext alert logging by setting:

```
output alert_fast: alerts.log
```

4. Enable pcap logging by setting:

```
output log_tcpdump: tcpdump.log
```

How it works...

Let's look at how Ubuntu configures logging, and then we'll make some additional adjustments in order to get more experience with some of the logging options.

Ubuntu stock

```
output unified2: filename snort.log, limit 128, nostamp, mpls_event_
types, vlan_event_types
```

Let's take a look at what those mean:

- ▶ unified2: The log format to use. Unified2 is a binary log format that provides the ability log with a choice of alert information, packet captures, or both.

- ▶ filename snort.log: This is exactly what it looks like: the name of the file which will be logged to. The filename is relative to the directory set in the environment variable LOGDIR, that on Ubuntu is set in /etc/default/snort.

- ▶ limit 128: This is the maximum allowed size of the log file in MB. The log file format is a circular buffer, so once 128MB of data has been logged, it starts overwriting the oldest data.

- ▶ nostamp: This defines if the log filename should have the current Unix timestamp appended to it when it is created. The default in the code is set to include the timestamp, but it is overridden by the configuration file's nostamp setting.

- ▶ mpls_event_types: If set, any MPLS labels on the network traffic will be logged as a part of the event.

- ▶ vlan_event_types: If set, any VLAN tags on the network traffic will be logged as part of the event.

Enable fast logging

This logging method accepts a filename to log to and an optional file size limit to override the default of 128MB. Once filled, a log rotation is triggered and a new `logfile` is created with the current timestamp appended. The log format is simple, only including alert ID, alert name, classification, and protocol, along with some basic IP/Port information from the connection.

Enabling Tcpdump logging

Much like fast logging, Tcpdump logging only accepts a filename and an optional file size limit. Rather than logging a text alert however, the IP packets relevant to the alert are logged in pcap format, which can easily be read by tcpdump or wireshark.

Other logging options

Some other options that Snort has for logging are:

- ▶ `alert_full`: Another text logging format similar to `alert_fast`, but it includes significantly more alert detail. So much so that it is not recommended for use, except on low traffic networks.

- ▶ `csv`: Allows you to log to comma-separated value (`csv`) files, which can easily be imported into a database.

- ▶ `log_null`: Allows you to disable the logging of packet captures, which is the equivalent of running Snort with `-N`. The alert instances themselves will still be triggered. This option provides more flexibility to using `-N`, since you can use `ruletype` definitions to limit the use of this output method to a subset of alert types.

- ▶ `alert_unixsock`: Allows you to log to a Unix domain socket that you create. This provides some flexibility for passing alerts to other applications.

Index

A

Active Directory requirements
  ability to manage DNS records 58
  about 58
  static IP address 58
  synchronized time 58
aliases
  setting up 76
Apache
  configuring, with TLS 46, 47
  WebDAV, configuring through 68, 69
Apache module
  used, for setting up PHP 49
Arp-Scan
  used, for detecting systems 113, 114
  working 115
authenticated access
  granting 65
authentication, for outbound e-mail
  configuring 81, 82
authnz_external configuration 70

B

Backup Domain Controller (BDC) 55
Bayesian Filtering 84
bind configuration
  about 59
  Apparmor rules changes 59
  dlz setting 59
  tkey-gssapi-keytab 59
  Zone updating 59

C

centralized logging
  input methods 124
  output methods 124, 125
  setting up 124
Core Rules Set (CRS) 51

D

defined ports
  forwarding, OpenSSH used 39, 40
DHCP
  global configuration parameters 11
  setting up 10-12
directory definition
  about 71
  authentication 71
  authorization 71
  basic Apache Directory configuration 72
  WebDAV, enabling 72
directory directive 70
DNS
  configuring, for XMPP 95, 96
DNS backends
  BIND9_DLZ 59
  BIND_FLATFILE 59
  SAMBA_INTERNAL 59
DNS records
  setting up, for e-mail delivery 78, 79
Domain Name System (DNS) 17
dynamic DNS
  configuring, on local network 21-23

T

TCP connect scan
  starting 116
TCP ports
  scanning 115-117
TCP SYN scan
  starting 116
Trunk 16

U

Ubuntu stock, Snort logging
  filename snort.log 131
  limit 128-131
  mpls_event_types 131
  nostamp 131
  unified2 131
  vlan_event_types 131
UDP ports
  scanning 117, 118
Unsolicited Commercial E-mail (UCE) 83
User Chat (MUC) rooms 99
users, Nagios
  adding 102, 103
  authentication 103
  authorization 103

V

VLAN tagging 14, 15

W

Web Application Firewall (WAF) 50
web applications
  securing, mod_security used 50, 51
WebDAV
  about 68
  configuring, through Apache 68, 69
  write access, granting 72
Windows Security IDs (SID) 61
worker MPM
  scaling, improving with 47-49

X

XMPP 87